Faces in the Revolution

FACES IN THE REVOLUTION

*The Psychological Effects of Violence
on Township Youth in South Africa*

GILL STRAKER

**with *Fathima Moosa,*
*Risé Becker & Madiyoyo Nkwale***

DAVID PHILIP: *Cape Town*
OHIO UNIVERSITY PRESS: *Athens*

To HETTY & WALLACE STRAKER

First published 1992 in southern Africa by David Philip Publishers (Pty) Ltd, 208 Werdmuller Centre, Claremont 7700, South Africa

Published 1992 in the United States of America by Ohio University Press, Scott Quadrangle, Athens, Ohio 45701, USA

ISBN 0-86486-203-2 (David Philip)
ISBN 0-8214-1040-7 (Ohio University Press)

© 1992 Gillian Straker

Printed by Belmor Book Printers, Cape Town, South Africa

Library of Congress Cataloging-in-Publication Data

Straker, Gill.
    Faces in the revolution : the psychological effects of violence on township children in South Africa / Gill Straker : in collaboration with Fathima Moosa.
        p.   cm.
    Includes bibliographical references and index.
    ISBN 0-8214-1040-7
    1. Youth—South Africa—Psychology—Longitudinal studies.
2. Violence—South Africa—Psychological aspects—Longitudinal studies.
3. Blacks—South Africa—Psychology—Longitudinal studies.
I. Moosa, Fathima. II. Title.
HQ799.S5S78 1992
305.23'0968—dc20   92-7049
                                                        CIP

Contents

Acknowledgements

In producing this book we are much indebted to a number of people and wish to extend an expression of gratitude to the following persons who have assisted with the preparation of this manuscript and with whose help it has been made possible:

The youth of Leandra who were willing to enter into dialogue with me and to share their thoughts and experiences.

Colleagues and friends who read this manuscript and provided useful comments and encouragement, especially Anne Moore, Tony Brink, Naomi Richman, Jo-Ann Loots, Bridie O'Driscoll, Pam Christie, Nell Robertson, Mary Cobbett, Elizabeth Elbert, Sue Brown and Robin Hornibrook.

Members of the Sanctuary Counselling Team and the South African Council of Churches.

Sanco Mulaudzi for help in translation.

Ursula Walters for opening channels of communication with the international community and for being a steadfast friend from afar.

Jean Gobey and the secretarial staff in the Psychology Department at the University of the Witwatersrand who helped with printing, photocopying and generally managing the dispersion of this document.

Ken Barris and Russell Martin for their editorial assistance.

Catholic Fund for Overseas Development, and Justice and Peace (Catholic Diocese of Johannesburg), for providing the financial assistance which made this project possible.

Royalties from this book will be used to further the education of the youth about whom this book has been written.

Foreword

'Violence is a monster which devours its own children,' wrote a Palestinian journalist who was horrified by what was happening to young people involved in the *Intifada* (*Weekly Mail,* 14–20 June 1991).

South Africans are struggling to come to terms with the violence of the past and present, whilst also attempting to fashion a different future where peace and justice can prevail. In doing so most people are pinning their hopes on a healing process which can cover the wounds of the past.

Violence has become like a festering sore in the body of South African society. It has undermined the fabric of our society. It bursts forth, pouring pus and blood just as we begin to have hope that temporary calm will become a true harbinger of peace.

It is very easy under such circumstances to think of violence in an institutional sense only and forget the individuals involved in it. Gill Straker's book is a timeous reminder to South Africans on both sides of the divide about the centrality of individuals in a violent society. Individual policemen and soldiers have been brutalised by the violence acts they have carried out in the name of state security. Similarly affected have been individual bureaucrats, government officials and indeed cabinet ministers, whose actions have constituted crimes against humanity equally as violent as physical force: removals, dispossessions, pass raids, denial of educational opportunities, and more.

Amongst the oppressed, violence has also become an acceptable survival strategy. Both revolutionary violence and ordinary criminal violence have attained a measure of legitimacy. Individuals are caught up in it too, and tortured by its brutalising effect.

For healing to occur, all South Africans will have to acknowledge the need for a healing process. Healing is likely to be difficult if one assumes that one can forget and forgive. The young people in this book are unlikely to forget. They may forgive, but forget they are unlikely to. It is also not healthy in a therapeutic sense to forget one's past: such forgetting would introduce dissonance, with serious consequences for long-term stability in social relations. The quality of social and interpersonal relations may also be negatively affected if people forget their past.

It is also unrealistic to expect forgiveness if one does not express remorse. Few white South African leaders have found it within their capacity to apologise for their complicity in apartheid. This lack of remorse is likely to impede the healing process. The goodwill and the capacity to forgive have been demonstrated by many responses to the public apologies of Leon Wessels and other people. It is a small price to pay for years of violent action against a people.

Most South Africans are both victims and perpetrators of violence. Gill Straker has a message of hope for all of us. There is a capacity for healing in most of us. Individually South Africans will have to struggle to find the best path to attain healing for themselves as individuals. So, too, society as a whole will have to find appropriate vehicles for facilitating healing. It may take a series of cleaning rituals in a variety of settings, but whatever its form we as individuals and as a society have to have the courage to go through the process of restoring wholeness to our societal fabric.

Dr M. A. RAMPHELE
University of Cape Town

Preface

When the manuscript of this book was put into my hands I began to skim through it. I soon became totally engrossed and was unable to put it down. No one that reads this book will remain the same.

The book is based on in-depth interviews with sixty Leandra activists ranging in age from 12 to 22 years. They had fled from their homes at the time of great upheaval in the mid-1980s and sought sanctuary in a church centre. The author made contact with the group as a counsellor, and a rapport was established with them. She shows great compassion and humanity towards these young people, but this has not devalued the scholarship of the project.

The study set out to explore in some depth the personalities and lives of each person in the group, to provide an alternative sense of how young people in this conflict situation see themselves.

The case-study format makes very interesting reading. It gives a deep insight into the problems and frustrations faced by the youth. In context, the turn to violence by the youth is partly understandable but no less frightening. Young people have paid a heavy price for their convictions. The author explains why she used the case-study method. 'In a time such as the present, when death, injury, pain and distress are being generated on an unprecedented scale, it is important to individualise this and to stress that each statistic has a name, a face and a family.'

People whose lives are untouched by violence and who are not exposed to the horrors which the township and hostel dwellers endure on a daily basis should read the book. For the profiles of these young people hold up a mirror to our society, moulded as they are by its violent culture and values. They have lived in townships that are characterised by overcrowding, few street lights and often no electricity. Most of the young interviewed have no stable family unit, many come from single-parent homes or homes with no parents at all. They had been left to the care of relatives and neighbours, deprived of opportunities for decent schooling, and drenched in a culture of violence with no positive role models.

The encouraging finding of this study is that youth are able to adapt to peace, despite their exposure to war, as various studies of other situations have concluded. Zimbabwe is cited as an example where a realignment of power within the families, schools and communities took place after the civil war. Gill Straker's findings make the appearance of this book important and timely because of the violence in which South Africa is at present engulfed. Behind the political question of charting the course of democracy looms the social crisis of black youth. They are very poor, uneducated, jobless and without skills. Straker's study will help us understand the scale of the problem we face in integrating these youth as productive citizens within the mainstream of national life.

Let me echo Gill Straker's final message: 'The needs of children and families must be a priority in any society, but where discriminatory social policies have been enshrined in laws actively undermining black family life, this takes on a particular urgency. Families remain at this point the most accessible and the most successful units for providing child care and they should thus be supported in all their diverse forms. For, in the final analysis, it will be the degree to which proper nurturance and care for all South African children is provided, and the degree to which they are socialised toward tolerance, which will determine the extent to which South African youth can be transformed from faces in a revolution to whole persons in a peaceful world.'

BRIGALIA BAM
Deputy General Secretary
South African Council of Churches

Introduction

In 1976 Soweto township erupted. Thousands of schoolchildren took to the streets in peaceful protest over inferior education. The police responded with armed force, and by the end of the year 176 were dead and more than a thousand injured.

The protest was not quelled. Though it subsided in the late 1970s, the revolt flared up again in 1980, and then in response to the exclusion of blacks from the new Constitution enacted in 1983, erupted in the mid-1980s with an unprecedented intensity. At its peak between 1984 and 1986, South Africa was in a state of civil war, and black youth were at the forefront of events. Young activists were involved in politicising the community, engineering work stay-aways, and enforcing consumer boycotts. When the state retaliated, the youth were exposed to brutal retribution. They responded with further violence, throwing petrol-bombs at administration buildings, erecting traps for armoured vehicles, attacking symbols of the state, and beating and sometimes killing blacks regarded as sellouts and collaborators.

It was at this time that the practice of 'necklacing' – immolating people by means of a rubber tyre placed round the neck, doused with petrol and set alight – became widespread. Many young people both witnessed and participated in these and other forms of violence. Simultaneously, large numbers were detained by state agencies, and allegedly tortured. Thousands more were harassed and attacked in their own homes and communities by members of the South African Police and South African Defence Force.

Human rights organisations were understandably outraged. American lawyers brought out a report on South Africa's war against children which was published in 1986. The Black Sash, a predominantly white liberal women's organisation, wrote a memorandum on the suffering children, and progressive professional bodies and the liberal press took up the cudgels in this cause. Concern was expressed about the effects of widespread political violence on the mental health of young people exposed to it. Quotes such as the following became common:

> Apartheid has brutalised a generation of children and given rise to fears of a Khmer Rouge situation in the country (*Sunday Star*, May 1987).

> These studies showed that, in the absence of rehabilitation work, there was every likelihood of the young growing up as militaristic automatons incapable of participating in their own destinies (*The Star*, April 1988).

> The sociopolitical climate placed such tremendous pressure on South Africans that the SA Institute of Clinical Psychology has warned of a generation of maladjusted children (*The Star*, October 1986).

> Youth are being tortured, detained, killed. This is one of the tragedies of this country that they [the youth] are being brutalised in this fashion and they are in turn brutalising others (Black Sash, 1986).

The explicit intention of the organisations and individuals that made these statements was to halt the devastation caused by apartheid, to protect black youth from further attacks by the state and to pressurise the state to put an end to violence. Many of the campaigns initiated by these human rights organisations, for example the Free the Children campaign, were extremely well run, and were highly successful in influencing international opinion.

One point of concern, however, was the negative image of black youth that these campaigns unwittingly projected. They were portrayed as the 'Khmer Rouge generation', 'Lords of the Flies', a broken, brutal mass, though there was little hard data to justify this depiction. On the home front this image lent itself to use and abuse by various hostile forces, including the state.

At the same time that the liberal press was reproducing images like these and inadvertently condemning black youth in the act of their defence, the state was presenting its own picture. It promoted primarily an image of youth as conspirators and revolutionaries or, paradoxically, as victims of manipulation by outside forces.

The comrades have over the past two years set up alternative systems in opposition to the official authorities as an instrument to promote revolutionary strategy.... The comrades have caused the disintegration of the official black municipalities through intimidation.... Their role is to destabilise order and then to fill the existing power vacuum with an alternative system (*The Star*, 21 September 1986).

In two separate trials, the state has claimed that the structures of administration which developed in Alexandra and elsewhere during 1986 (set up in part by politically mobilised youth) were aimed at developing organs of people's power and undermining institutions of state power such as the supreme court, police and local authorities (G. Moss, *Work in Progress*, July 1987).

In depicting the youth as conspirators and revolutionaries in this way, the state attempted to justify its use of repressive measures. The youth involved, however, took on none of these images. They projected themselves as freedom fighters and heroes. Their view of themselves was encapsulated in the slogans they embraced, such as 'Freedom or Death – Victory is Certain' and 'Forward to People's Power'.

Professional and mental health organisations were ill-prepared for the crisis of the mid-1980s. Staffed largely by white middle-class personnel and trained in the 'treatment' of 'disturbed' and 'problematic' individuals, they were not equipped to deal with the large numbers of persons requiring diverse forms of help who presented themselves in the wake of the civil strife. Their first response was to attempt to modify the knowledge they had, in a bid to provide an appropriate service. Reflections upon these events, as well as systematic research, came much later. Valuable opportunities to address a variety of crucial questions were lost.

Among these questions one might number the following: Who joins the struggle and why? Through what processes are they inducted into the struggle? What factors sustain their participation in the struggle? To what extent have they both been subjected to and participated in violence? What seems to be the effects of this involvement in violence? What are the implications for the future? This book is an attempt, in retrospect, to answer some of these questions.

In 1986 I was approached to provide counselling to a group of sixty youth who had been forced to flee township violence and had sought sanctuary in a church centre, the Wilgespruit Fellowship Centre. The aid of nine other mental health professionals was enlisted and the Sanctuary Counselling Team, operating under the auspices of the South African Council of Churches (SACC), was launched. The main brief of this team was to provide services to youth traumatised and displaced by political violence.

During the initial phases of this endeavour we, as a group of counsellors, suffered the secondary trauma so well described in disaster psychiatry literature. At the time we were too overwhelmed to realise this, with some disastrous consequences. Nor did we realise that soon hundreds and thousands of refugees from all over the country would be forced to flee mounting violence in South Africa's townships.

This study is an attempt to describe the original group of young- sters whose flight from the township of Leandra in 1986 led to the launch of the Sanctuary Counselling Programme. Much of the mater- ial is reconstructed retrospectively from interviews conducted some months later with the refugees, and from interviews with counsel- lors, house parents and field workers.

In addition, with the help of two researchers I undertook a follow-up study of the group in 1989. With some difficulty, most of the original group were located, and in-depth interviews were con- ducted with about 40 per cent of them to find out what had hap- pened to them in the intervening period. Their experiences during 1984–1989 were explored, as were their reflections upon these events.

This book, therefore, is based on the accounts of people inti- mately involved in South Africa's struggle for freedom. It is a study in which all participants brought their diverse personal perspectives to the events which occurred, reflecting many of the key images of youth described above. In the final analysis, however, it represents my own reading of the situation, a distillation of data reflected in some 300 hours of recorded interviews.

Four intentions have informed this account. Firstly, in answering the questions discussed above, I hope that the diversity of trauma which many South African youth suffer may be placed in context and understood more clearly.

The second intention is to explore in some depth the personalities and the lives of individuals in the group. The concerns of this book are therefore individual and psychological rather than sociological and historical.

The third intention is to explore, in the context of the psychological literature on violence, the claims made by the liberal press that a brutal generation has been spawned in South Africa; specifically, to consider the question of whether violence begets violence and to provide an alternative sense of how young black people in South Africa's conflict-torn townships see themselves.

The fourth intention is to examine the factors that contribute to both the psychological vulnerability and the psychological resilience of youth at war.

1 Trauma in War

Over the past fifteen years a number of human rights organisations have monitored the extent to which conflict and violence have become endemic in South Africa. During 1986 alone, the Detainees' Parents Support Committee estimated that approximately 10 000 children, some as young as ten and eleven years, were detained in jails. Allegations of torture and intimidation were commonplace. In addition, troops occupied many of the townships and intervened in the civil life of the young. Schools were frequently surrounded and access was strictly controlled. Troops supervised examinations and enforced discipline, often brutally. Between 1984 and 1986, figures show that 300 children were killed by the police and military, 1 000 wounded, 18 000 arrested on charges relating to political protest, and 173 000 held in police cells awaiting trial (Swartz & Levett, 1989). In addition, there was an increase in vigilante violence and in all forms of counter-violence. Children in the townships were thus living in a state of civil war (DPSC, 1986, p.114–141). Under these conditions it is difficult to retain one's concern for the individual as the statistics steadily mount. Yet each statistic has a name, a face, a history and a family.

This chapter therefore focuses not on the general but on the particular. It presents the experiences of a group of youths from the township of Leandra who were subjected over a six-week period to a succession of incidents of trauma, all of which would be classified as catastrophic by mental health workers using standard diagnostic criteria. Their history is not claimed to be representative of the experiences of youth in all townships, or even all youth in Leandra. Nevertheless it would seem that these experiences are not unique and that the insights gleaned from them have an applicability beyond Leandra. Furthermore, a description of the events in Leandra gives a context within which to understand the complexity of the conflicts which the system of apartheid has spawned.

These conflicts pertain not only to the actions of the South African Defence Force and Police against the community but to splits within the community, such as those between conservatives and progressives, young and old, haves and have-nots, and between different anti-apartheid groups. The last-mentioned are natural and inevitable, but they have been exploited by the state to promote what it has termed 'black-on-black' violence. This term, intended as it is to convey visions of warring black tribes and factions locked in battle, in which their innate aggression and brutality is expressed, has to a large extent been successful in obscuring the true origins of violence within the black community.

In describing the events in Leandra which preceded the outbreak of violence in the township, the degree to which general apartheid policies resulted in, promoted and sustained this violence will become clear. The study will also highlight how in the Leandra episode this conflict was rooted in the government's policy of forced removal of whole communities.

The violence that erupted in Leandra was not only historically rooted in apartheid policies but, once it started, its intensity was sustained by police action or, rather, police inaction at the time. This pattern of selective involvement of the police in inter-group conflicts has been reported in numerous townships. Similarly, the state's exploitation of the mistakes made by anti-apartheid organisations in Leandra reflects a pattern which has been repeated in various other centres across the country. It is hoped therefore that the complexity of some of the conflicts in South Africa and the diversity of the trauma generated will become clearer in our discussion.

Leandra is a township near Secunda in the Eastern Transvaal, and is also known as Mpumelelo. It is relatively small, but particularly squalid. As one approaches it in the early morning, a blanket of smog enshrouds the area. Very few of the houses have electricity, and even these are not very large or particularly attractive, but they are at least functional. In this way they differ from the hundreds of cast-iron shacks that surround them. These have no running water, electricity or piped sewerage. They are reliant on the bucket system and given the level of overcrowding, the overflow of night-soil is a frequent occurrence. This adds to the mess of garbage which litters the streets. At almost any time of the day people can be seen with large plastic containers balanced on wheelbarrows or laboriously carried to and from communal taps. They pick their way through garbage and litter down paths which are either dusty or muddy, depending on the season. In summer it is oppressively hot; there are very few trees to provide shade. In winter it is often bitterly cold. Regardless of the season, however, much of Leandra remains a health hazard and an eyesore, ugly, dirty and smelly. In short, it is a thoroughly unpleasant place to live in.

Yet it is a township which until the end of 1984 had been united in its opposition to a government threat to relocate the population forcibly (Haysom, 1986). In the early 1980s, the government was still committed to its homeland policy of creating separate 'independent states' for black people along ethnic lines. In terms of this policy, it wished to re-locate much of the population of Leandra to the homeland of KwaNdebele. The state thus proposed a renewal scheme for Leandra in terms of which new accommodation would be provided for permit holders, or people who qualified for urban resident status. '"Lodgers" – usually the extended family of the permit holder – were to be thrown out of their homes, which were torn apart, and occupants forced into small shacks on the fringe of the township' (Haysom, 1986, p. 3). The authorities at first indicated that this action against 'lodgers' was to be temporary and that they too would be accommodated. It was not long, however, before threats were made to evict a few of these families. Conflict broke out between the police and residents, and four people were dead within a few hours (Haysom, 1986). This contributed to rising tensions within the community.

The Leandra Action Committee (LAC), which had been formed to fight off forced relocation, took up cudgels on behalf of those who did not have resident status, the 'outsiders'. This committee was headed by Chief Ampie Mayisa, a township leader who believed that the community should remain united against the state and the black local councillors, and that it should not be influenced by promises to upgrade the houses of the outsiders. In supporting the outsiders Chief Mayisa antagonised a large number of the insiders who had developed a vested interest in the *status quo*.

This conflict was exacerbated when the Leandra Action Committee announced that it was to affiliate to the United Democratic Front (UDF), an umbrella organisation for a great many bodies committed to fighting the apartheid regime.

In Leandra, as in most townships in South Africa, large numbers of youth supported the UDF. These 'comrades' were fully in favour of the LAC affiliating with the UDF, and an alliance between the youth and the LAC was therefore cemented. When in 1985 there was a national schools boycott, Leandra students took part, even though they were poorly organised and not wholly united in this decision. The split in their ranks became clearer later when members of the LAC and a group of parents met and decided that it was now time for the students to return to school. A number of the youth refused to do this and were supported in their view by comrades from neighbouring townships who felt that the boycott should continue. They intimidated students who wished to return to school and behaved in a generally threatening and undisciplined fashion. As these youth were associated with the LAC, their behaviour strengthened the hand of those opposed to Chief Mayisa and the LAC, who were accused of having no control over their supporters.

The students who wished to return to school were approached at this time by Mayboy Zondo, leader of a conservative faction in the township, who offered them accommodation and protection. Because the comrades had antagonised many in the community, especially parents and older people through their lack of discipline, Zondo at first won some popular support. It soon became clear however that his ambitions extended beyond the students to taking control of the township by ousting Chief Mayisa and those sympathetic to the LAC and the UDF. Zondo and his group began a campaign of violence against Mayisa and those who supported him, including the comrades, which culminated in Mayisa's brutal murder early in 1986. His slaying was to make obvious the link between Zondo's vigilante group and the state.

On 11 January 1986, Mayisa, realising that he was about to be attacked, phoned the Leandra police to report that his house was under siege and that he required assistance. A record of this phone call was later seen by Richard Spoor, an articled clerk employed by Priscilla Jana, the attorney acting for the Mayisa family. Spoor indicated in an affidavit that the call was investigated by Sergeant Ras of the Leandra uniformed branch, who reported the situation to a Lieutenant Slabbert of the Riot Squad. Despite the request for help, and the severity of the situation as confirmed by subsequent events, Slabbert instructed the police to remain on the outskirts of the township.

Earlier incidents of assault on Mayisa and his supporters had also been reported to the police but these too had not been responded to effectively (Haysom, 1986). The police therefore were tacitly involved in the violence which erupted and culminated in the death of Chief Ampie Mayisa in January 1986. It should also be said that Mayisa's murderers were never convicted.

Mayisa's slaying was violent in the extreme; it was to this murder that the group of youth who are the subject of this book was exposed. Some of them were in the house when it took place; they witnessed the prelude to his death, including a petrol-bomb attack. Their descriptions of these events were largely in accord with those given subsequently in an affidavit by a witness, Lucas Mbonane, who claimed he had been forced to join the mob that killed Mayisa (Haysom, 1986).

On the day he was murdered, Mayisa was in a meeting with a number of comrades and parents discussing the conflict in the township, when his house was surrounded by approximately a hundred vigilantes who called for Mayisa to come out. When he did not emerge, a petrol-bomb was flung at the house. The group inside scattered and fled. Mayisa himself ran and hid in a disused truck where he was trapped by the vigilantes. He was attacked with axes and knives and was stabbed and hacked to death. His body was badly mutilated and his daughters were subsequently told that his genitals had been severed. After this, the body was taken to a scrapyard and burned (Haysom, 1986).

Two weeks later Mayisa was buried. The vigilantes gathered in small bands along the funeral route. When a person whom the mourners believed to be a vigilante was seen in the vicinity of the service itself, violence broke out. A band of eighty mourners attacked and killed the suspected vigilante. Shortly after this, a group of fifty vigilantes engaged the mourners in hand-to-hand combat. A police vehicle was said to have driven past but to have ignored the proceedings. The situation steadily deteriorated, both on the day of the funeral and subsequently. As many as 300 children and adolescents were estimated to have fled the area. Many of the children sought refuge with the South African Council of Churches, which placed them in the shelter of the Wilgespruit Fellowship Centre.

The following account by Mary Cobbett, a worker at the community centre, of the arrival of the youth and their attempts to adjust to the situation gives a sense of the difficulties encountered:

> My first contact with this group from Leandra was a phone call from the SACC requesting that we provide accommodation for

some refugees for two or three days. They started coming, in groups of five or six, until there were about 55. Not all the children were from Leandra; a few were from neighbouring townships.

We had them with us for two to three weeks. During this time I had very little interaction with them and they kept very much to themselves; we were expecting them to return home any moment. I also could not understand the language although some of them did speak a bit of English.

Then one day they didn't turn up for breakfast and subsequently didn't arrive for lunch. On investigation it appeared that they were going to boycott meals because of various frustrations and grievances. I then held a meeting. (At that point there were about 55 to 60 children. They were all living in the chapel because Wilgespruit was very full and we did not have other accommodation for them, and besides, we were under the impression that they were soon to leave.) They had a large list of complaints that they wanted to discuss; the most important one was that they wanted separate accommodation for the boys and girls. They'd been up the night before singing songs all night because 'they did not want to lie down together', as they put it. They didn't like the food, or the way they had to come to meals, and sometimes they had to come in late because there were many people at Wilgespruit doing courses who ate before they did.

They suggested that they set up a crisis committee and asked if I would recognise it. I said that I would be delighted to. We then began planning how to help them to solve their problems as it had become clear to me that they would be here for a while.

The first thing I did was to apply to the Bishop for two timber huts which we were subsequently granted. We also established committees to deal with a variety of problems, namely a discipline committee, a health and hygiene committee, and so on. I think things could have worked out quite well, but I really only had a week to work with them on those committees before the police raided.

The youth had been at the community centre for approximately two weeks when it was invaded by the police. They arrived heavily armed, in cars and helicopters equipped with searchlights. Some of the youth attempted to flee and two were shot and wounded. A few escaped, but the others were arrested. As Mary Cobbett relates:

> It was 6 o'clock in the morning when we heard the sound of helicopters coming in low. We were still in bed at the time. Billy and I jumped up and got dressed and left the baby – she was sleeping. Billy ran out towards the chapel from where gunshots could be heard. I ran off down to the kitchen and the dining-hall. The black staff were all in there and they asked me to go to their staff houses and tell their children to stay indoors, which I did. As I ran down to the staff houses the police were approaching. It seemed like an army of them. They were carrying machine-guns but they didn't challenge me; I just ran right past them.
>
> But when I went into the black staff houses I drew the attention of the police to those inside because two policemen followed me in. I insisted that the children present belonged to the staff. They then proceeded to search them and open and search everything. One of the sons of a staff member, who was 18 years old, was detained; they told him to get dressed.
>
> As I came out of the staff houses two plain-clothes police-men were standing near the lower dormitory and I thought they were ... well, I'd been waiting for a group to arrive the night before and they didn't turn up and I asked: 'Are you from one of the groups?' They certainly weren't.
>
> All the girls were shrieking and I tried to calm them down and told them to get dressed quickly. I'd been away from my house for about half an hour and I wanted to get back. So I ran back to my house and by that time Billy had come back. The police came through our house but they didn't search it and didn't ask to look at anything. They just went into the office next to the house and began searching it. It didn't seem as if they knew particularly what they were looking for. And while this was going on, I could see the children being brought from in front of the dining-hall, past the office window, into the car park, to those police vans. They had the children outside and were rounding them up; I could also see squatters who had been brought in from the vicinity; the police were also bringing in people I did not even recognise, from the surrounding fields.

In our presence the police had been very polite and restrained. I went over to the kitchen where I discovered that their behaviour with the black kitchen staff had been completely different. When they had gone to search the single rooms, they had prevented Carol from getting dressed and she'd had to stand there naked. And Abel, who was in the habit of keeping his spade under his bed because tools always go missing and that is the safest place to put it, was accused of using it for hiding things; when Abel denied it they hit his son on the head and chest with the spade. They had gone into Peter's house and hit his sister. They had also strip-searched the housekeeper, Julia. I was quite horrified at the difference in police behaviour towards whites and blacks, and I thought: This was how it is! The reality of life in South Africa!

On my way to the kitchen, one of the squatters approached and said that someone had been shot; the victim was in the bush at the squatter camp. As some of the policemen had gone over the hill we were worried that they were watching us, so I asked the squatter to tell the wounded person to try to crawl under cover to my office where I would meet him. And then one of the members said that there was also someone in the toilet who was hurt. We needed a doctor but we were terrified the police would come back. We couldn't go to the hospital because the police put pressure on the staff there to report wounded people who turn up, so we had to find a safe doctor. We eventually managed to do this. We then started legal proceedings to get the children released and after some days and a court interdict, we achieved this.

After their release from jail, the youth made a number of statements concerning their treatment in the days following their arrest. Many of the boys complained that they had been taken to a number of different jails. They complained that they had been beaten and deprived of food. Some alleged that they had been taken back to Leandra and the vigilantes who attacked them previously had been let into their cells. They did not, however, complain of torture or extreme maltreatment except Mandla, whose feet were badly injured by hammering with a rifle butt. Some of the girls too were very distressed and complained that they had been given injections forcibly, which seemed more upsetting to them than anything else.

In the week following the return of the youth to the centre, the staff were too busy dealing with individual problems to cope effectively with the group as a whole.

In general the youth were very restless and agitated. Their whole relationship to Wilgespruit was conflict-ridden. Although they had originally gone there voluntarily and had seen it as a place of safety, after their arrest and the application by the Wilgespruit staff for a court interdict to have them returned, they began to suspect staff members of acting in collaboration with the state. This situation was aggravated by the fact that some of the workers at Wilgespruit belonged to a different anti-apartheid group, the Azanian People's Organisation (AZAPO), while the youth belonged to the UDF. In the townships the conflict between these two groups is intense, and so these various affiliations did not help matters when the group returned to Wilgespruit with levels of suspicion and hostility already extremely high.

The group at this point was understandably obsessed with the issue of security. They were worried about Wilgespruit being invaded again. They felt trapped but had nowhere else to go, for it was not safe to return to the township. They were also concerned about their families who, they feared, were being harassed by the police and the vigilantes. Furthermore, they were anxious that the vigilantes might attack Wilgespruit either directly or indirectly through the use of witchcraft and sorcery. The group as a whole expressed a fear that the vigilantes had engaged a very powerful sorcerer to undermine and subvert them. Lastly, the collective anxiety and guilt the group felt over the death of Mayisa expressed itself in shared nightmares that Mayisa was haunting them and that he would not rest or allow them peace until his severed genitals had been united with his body.

In order to deal with the group's anxiety that they had been bewitched by the vigilantes, religious leaders such as Bishop Nkoane (the Anglican Bishop Suffragan of Johannesburg and a member of the SACC) were called in to perform ritual exorcisms. It was also at this point that the help of the counsellors who later con- stituted the Sanctuary Counselling Team was sought. The initial task of the counsellors was to address the nightmares and insomnia con- nected to the trauma of Mayisa's death. A therapy programme was designed to alleviate the group's guilt about its failure to protect Mayisa. This programme, along with the exorcisms, seemed to work at least temporarily in that the nightmares and the shared group paranoia abated.

However, the group's realistic anxieties about the security at Wilgespruit persisted. In order to deal with this, it was arranged that the youths would all be taken away for a week to an alternative sanctuary, where a very structured programme had been organised to help the group work through some of the trauma of the preceding weeks as well as to plan for the future. The results of this move were disastrous. The anxiety and hostility in the group escalated. Once at the new centre they insulted the staff, were intimidating in their behaviour, and demanded to be taken back to Wilgespruit immediately. When they threatened to hijack the bus that had transported them there, one of the staff had to sleep in it to prevent this.

In view of the distress that the move created, it was decided to return to Wilgespruit the next day. On their return, the group indicated a willingness to discuss their problems. However, they remained volatile and there were several incidents of aggression against staff members. On one occasion members of the group threw food on the floor in protest at the allegedly poor quality. On a second occasion some members of the group surrounded one of the kitchen staff and threatened to burn her unless she provided them with cigarettes. A member of the counselling team was aggressively accused of being an informer. In yet another incident, two of the residential staff workers were physically threatened following an altercation over discipline, which arose over the smoking of marijuana by certain individuals in the group.

By this time the group had been at Wilgespruit about eight weeks and its composition and structure had altered. Many of the leaders had not returned after the police raid, either because they were still detained or because they were amongst those who had escaped. In addition, new splinter groups had arrived in the meantime from Leandra and from other townships, creating crises of leadership and disrupting existing alliances. Furthermore, there were differing levels of politicisation and differences of opinion about how the time at Wilgespruit should be spent. Some members felt that discipline should be maintained and the time should be spent studying and preparing for their return. Others felt this was time for relaxation and recreation. Violence broke out and various sub-groups assaulted one another. When the staff intervened and expelled those they saw as the culprits, the group threatened the staff, and community leaders had to be called in to try to contain the situation. The outcome of the consultations with the community leaders was that the youth themselves agreed that staying at Wilgespruit was becoming counterproductive and that together they needed to plan a strategy for their return home. It was also agreed that a meeting with the parents should be called to determine the degree of safety in the township.

The initial meeting with the parents was poorly attended. There were two reasons for this: firstly, the parents had difficulty in getting past the vigilantes when leaving the township; and secondly, many of the parents felt that their children were safer at Wilgespruit than in Leandra and were understandably not keen for them to return. However, it was finally agreed under a great deal of pressure from the group that they would go back. The parents were asked to try as best they could to mobilise supportive networks and to prepare the community for their children's home-coming. The children were to catch a train and then to arrange taxis to take them back to Leandra.

On their arrival by train at Springs, the group went to the police station to ask for an escort into the township, as it was suspected that the vigilantes might attack. The police, however, only agreed to escort them to the edge of the township; they refused to go in. As the group entered the township they were attacked. One girl was stabbed and one of the boys was assaulted and needed stitches. The rest fled and gradually filtered back to Wilgespruit.

The staff immediately called a press conference and another parents' meeting, which was very well attended. The parents now realised the youth were determined to come home and that they must accept this and prepare for it. For their part, the youth felt let down by their parents and indicated that it was vital that real preparations be made for their return.

It is doubtful whether the youth would ever have been able to return to Leandra had there not been a dramatic turn of events. About ten days after the abortive attempt to return, a small group captured a vigilante by the name of Moki outside the court where a case of public violence against them – subsequently to be dismissed – was being heard. Moki thereafter agreed to give evidence on behalf of the group and went into hiding. This provoked a backlash in Leandra, with the vigilantes and especially their leader, Mayboy Zondo, harassing and intimidating the group's families, and organising a campaign of hostility. By this time the link between the vigilantes and the state had been formalised: some of Zondo's followers were in the process of becoming municipal policemen. The situation was therefore critical for the group.

However, the capture of the vigilante proved to be a turning-point in the balance of power. According to one of the Wilgespruit staff, once Mayboy Zondo knew that Moki had been captured, he contacted the Leandra and Krugersdorp police for help. But Moki was not at Wilgespruit; he was in hiding.

Once again the group at Wilgespruit was subjected to various forms of harassment: a helicopter hovering overhead at night, two whites in a car trespassing and firing off shots, a dawn visit by two police vans bristling with policemen. One of the vigilantes phoned Wilgespruit and threatened an attack. The youth were petrified, and even staff members were intimidated. A meeting was called and it was decided to evacuate the place; it was cleared within five hours and the children were placed at alternative venues. Staff members left as well.

In the meantime a lawyer representing Wilgespruit suggested that Moki should come out of hiding and make a statement to the effect that he was not being held against his will and that he was going to give evidence. After this was done, matters began to change. Mayboy Zondo realised that Moki was serious and that the whole matter had gone beyond Leandra and the Leandra police. He then fled, as did some of the others. Without leadership, the vigilantes were left in disarray and the Wilgespruit staff felt they should seize the opportunity to return the Leandra group to the township.

This time no attempt was made to send the group back *en masse* but individuals were returned either singly or in small groups until all but the leaders had been returned. This proved a successful strategy, and apart from two of the leaders who had to go into hiding permanently, the members of the group were able to remain in Leandra, though two of them were killed subsequently. This underlines once more the violence and chaos endemic to South African society.

The events which occurred in Leandra are not unique to it, nor are the experiences of the group of youth after they had fled the township. The Leandra case-study illustrates some of the techniques used by agents of the state to undermine township unity and destabilise organisational structures. It shows how they exploit a situation of scarcity of resources by creating competition and how they then recruit people from within the community to fight their battles by proxy. They fan the fires of enmity that are already present and stand on the side-lines lending support to conservative forces but as far as possible avoiding direct engagement in the conflict. The success of this strategy in escalating and maintaining lack of unity, which undermines concerted resistance to the state, is clear. This strategy, it would seem, is still employed in the 1990s, despite the new era which speaks of negotiating. Yet however pertinent this investigation of Leandra may be to understanding the violence that still exists in South Africa, the intention of this study remains individual and psychological rather than sociological and historical. The following chapter therefore deals with the Leandra youth in psychological terms. It examines what kinds of people join the struggle, through what processes they are inducted into it, and what sustains them in struggle.

2 Psychological Resilience of Youth at War

It was a fairly widespread assumption, at least among whites, that the uprisings in the townships of 1984–86 did not have popular support. It was believed that they reflected the agitation and intimidation of the masses by a few troublemakers. The belief is incorrect. The truth is that the period was one of mass resistance in South Africa's black townships. Certainly among the youth it was the majority who participated in the eruptions. The youngster who did not participate in these popular uprisings was the exception rather than the rule.

Across the country, youth were observing school boycotts, enforcing consumer boycotts on their sometimes reluctant parents, burning city councillors' houses and their own schools, both of which were perceived to be symbols of apartheid, and engaging in street warfare with the police who responded with teargas, sjamboks, rubber bullets, buckshot and occasionally live ammunition. Young black people were detained, arrested and tortured. The declaration of the State of Emergency, which was put in place in 1985 and renewed in 1986, was official acknowledgement by the government of the full extent of popular resistance.

From the perspective of the youth, this was a time of euphoria as well as terror. They had a newfound sense of power and a vision for the future. They saw themselves as leading the older generation to freedom. Liberation was believed to be in sight and they were to be the authors of it. Many parents, however, were distressed by the militancy of the young, whose ideals might have been admirable, but they resented having these views forcibly imposed on them. They also feared for the safety and well-being of their children.

The white population struggled to make sense of what was happening. Aided by the media, they generated their own explanations of events: the unrest was orchestrated by communists; it was only supported by a minority of blacks, while the majority wanted the restoration of law and order, and longed to be rescued from the disorder and violence perpetrated by agitators and criminal elements. Clearly this understanding was not uniformly subscribed to, and there were alternative explanations of the unrest which focused on discrimination, economic deprivation and the political exclusion of blacks. However, the sentiment was widely shared that the sweeping collective protest was orchestrated by agitators from outside the country, and carried out by criminals and marginalised persons within.

In expounding these views, South African whites echoed similar explanations put forward in the wake of the riots which spread through the American ghettos of the 1960s and 1970s. In the USA, these views were soon shown to be fallacious. The Kerner Commission, a national committee set up to investigate the riots, soon concluded that 'to contend that the riots sprang from sophisticated organisational efforts was to take refuge in fantasy instead of fact' (quoted in Allen, 1970, p. 3). The 'riff-raff theory', which proposed that the criminal element was predominantly responsible for civil strife and rioting, was similarly discredited. Social scientists who carried out large-scale surveys and interviewed ghetto dwellers concluded that it was a myth that only a fraction of those in the riot area had participated. It was likewise a myth that the overwhelming majority of black Americans disapproved of the riots. On the contrary there was widespread sympathy and support among American blacks across the country for the riots, which were seen as one means of forcing the establishment to recognise the unacceptability of their lot (Allen, 1970; Caplan & Paige, 1968; Tomlinson, 1968). There was widespread legitimation of riots as a form of protest. Thus, citing the actions of *agents provocateurs* as the cause of the riots was totally fallacious, unless one was 'willing to call the mood of the people by that name' (Tomlinson, 1968, p. 29).

A large majority of investigators concluded further that the primary cause of the riots was the social climate endemic in American society in the 1950s and 1960s; it fostered a situation in which a riot response need not be created, but only disinhibited; the predisposition had already been created by existing social conditions (Tomlinson, 1968). Sophisticated analyses of the exact triggers of this disinhibition were presented in historical, political and sociological terms, as researchers attempted to explain both the timing and the specific location of the riots; patterns of urbanisation and particular economic developments were examined in great detail as social scientists sought to understand the events.

These analyses clearly have a bearing on what happened in South Africa in 1984–86, as do similar local analyses of the sociological, historical, political and economic variables involved. By and large, however, these studies fail to explore the psychological concomitants, which also have a place in the evolving pattern of events.

In drawing attention to international studies I do not, however, intend to suggest that the social and historical conditions in these countries necessarily paralleled those in South Africa. In many instances there were vast differences. Nevertheless, the psychological processes involved often showed similarities. As has already been seen in the American studies on the civil rights movement, one commonality of note was the shared response of sectors of the white public to these events. There are obvious reasons why the white public in both countries favoured explanations of civil disorder which attributed the causes of riots to individual pathology or to a conspiracy theory rather than to structural problems within the system. The conspiracy theory holds out the hope of deflecting blame for the problem from society itself, and has the potential to unite large sections of the population against an externalised enemy. Individualised explanations likewise hold out the hope that the situation can be contained without the necessity for real change. The troublemakers can be isolated, and the marginalised and criminal element can be imprisoned or rehabilitated.

However, what little research there is on activists refutes this representation. Although the ranks of resistance movements may at times be swelled by criminals and drop-outs who use the situation to their own advantage, these individuals are seldom the leaders or the initiators of such movements. Rather it is the more highly functioning, intelligent and socially sophisticated individuals who are at the forefront. Furthermore, as a group, militants have been found to have a greater sense of personal effectiveness than non-militants, who speak of greater feelings of powerlessness (Allen, 1970). Several studies have shown that militants are not those persons who are most socially, educationally or economically deprived. They are frequently better educated than non-militants. They are better integrated into the community, both socially and politically, and certainly the militant groups are not found to contain a higher percentage of deviants or criminals than the non-militant group

(Tomlinson, 1968).

In the view of Caplan and Paige (1968), who conducted extensive research in the United States, the central aspect which differentiates rioters from non-rioters is the former's refusal to accept discrimination as inevitable and their consequent rejection of passive adaptation to it. They suggested that rioters have abandoned the stereotype that makes non-achievement and acceptance of their lot the natural order of events. Rioters have negotiated a crucial psychological shift in perception from blaming the self for failure to perceiving causes in the social structure, while at the same time maintaining a sense of personal effectiveness. In her study of South African activists, Maluleke (1989) found that a similar psychological shift had been negotiated by those most active in the struggle in this country.

However, Maluleke's study, like much of the research in the United States, is not longitudinal and it relies heavily on a single interview. While there are some longitudinal studies in the international literature, they are relatively rare. Certainly in South Africa there is almost no longitudinal research in the area. The present study is an attempt to bridge this gap. It focuses on the personal characteristics of those who joined the struggle: the individuals in their social context, the processes whereby they were inducted into the struggle, those factors which sustained them in it, and those which might have pushed them beyond their ability to cope.

THE LEADERS

Ricky

At the time of the follow-up interview Ricky was nineteen years old. He is short and stocky, but lithe; his body has a certain tension about it. His face is expressive. Intense emotion as well as warmth and charm is expressed in his eyes as his discussions range over diverse topics. He is very alert. He continually assesses me and attempts to read cues of my intentions, strengths and vulnerabilities.

I do not have a sense that he is trying to read these cues so he can conform to my expectations. There is nothing obsequious or even placatory in his bearing. I rather have the sense that he is trying to read me in order to keep control of the terrain. He clearly sees me as a resource person. Underneath his charm and engaging manner, I sense a shrewd observer of human nature.

Ricky is charismatic. He knows how to win people over. Despite his pragmatic stance toward the world, he is not lacking in genuine warmth and concern. His involvement with and love of his family are obvious, as is his commitment to his community. He was born in Springs, which is some fifty kilometres from Leandra, where he currently lives. He has had many changes of residence in his short life, but his grandmother has remained the constant caretaker.

While he and his three siblings were growing up they saw relatively little of either parent. His mother was a live-in domestic worker who only returned home once a month. His father also stayed at his place of work, which was a considerable distance from Leandra.

Although he saw relatively little of either of his parents, Ricky reports that his memories of both are very pleasant. His most enduring memory of his mother is of her monthly return to his grandmother's house:

> We would wait for her. She always came with a packet filled with large brown scones. I remember those scones. The taste was so sweet and they were so big; my mouth was too small to get around them. When she had to leave she was very sad. She would give us sweets so we would not think of her going. She would place them before us and tell us she would be back soon. Then she would sneak out. We would wait for her but she would not come back for a long time.

He claims that his father was different from the fathers of many of his friends. He was strict but would never hit them before fully discussing their misdemeanour and the reasons for their punishment. Whenever he came to visit, he brought clothes and food for the family. He was an outspoken person, one who had the courage of his convictions. Ricky describes him as someone who was not cowed by government officials and whites. In fact he was killed when Ricky was fourteen years old, in a conflict with his white employers.

After his death, the family's financial position deteriorated drastically. They never starved, and neither he nor his siblings were forced to leave school to attempt to support the family, but they struggled to make ends meet. His father's death reinforced for Ricky a sense of the injustice of the circumstances governing the lives of blacks in South Africa. This sense had been fostered in him from a very young age by his grandmother, whom he remembers as an assertive woman, a leader in the community, and a great storyteller. Every night she would tell them traditional tales, for example of the

fox and the monkey and their various wiles; but she would also tell
them stories of her own life, such as her presence at the signing of
the Freedom Charter, or of the march on Pretoria of 50 000 women
to protest against the laws introduced to force women, like men, to
carry passes aimed at restricting freedom of movement into the
urban areas. She would show the children her *'dompas'* (the
detested pass permitting blacks to enter white areas for a limited
time) and tell them that they were to inherit her personal *dompas* to
remind them of their duty to fight for freedom. She described the
massacre at Sharpeville of 1960 and spoke of people she knew who
were connected with Mandela. Thus inspired, Ricky's political education was initiated at a very young age within the family circle.

In 1983, when Ricky was thirteen years old, a particularly significant incident occurred during state attempts to remove the residents
of Leandra by force. In that climate of fear and anger, he remembers
his mother courageously standing up to a black policeman, telling
him that he was a government stooge.

It was then that Ricky made personal contact with Abel Nkabinde
and Chief Ampie Mayisa, community leaders in Leandra. These two
men came to be key influences in his life. He attended meetings at
their houses, and his understanding of the issues in the township
deepened. When the Leandra Action Committee, which had been
formed to fight forced removals, allied itself with the United
Democratic Front, Ricky was totally supportive of the initiative. A
youth congress was established in the township at the same time
and he was elected to the executive.

In reflecting on this period, he recalls these times as heady ones.
There was a sense of euphoria in the township, especially among
the youth, experienced for example in visiting door to door to
explain campaigns and stayaways to as many people as possible – a
sense that the initiative was theirs.

Several key events stand out for him. These include the day it was
decided to attack the houses of all the local councillors, attacks in
which he participated. Another such event was the daylight raid on
a white-owned store on the outskirts of the township. He points out
that most of the local people took part in these episodes. There was
a sense of shared purpose, a feeling in the crowd that at last they
were standing up for their rights and being effective.

When Ricky was fifteen, like many other youths at the time, he set
up his own smaller group of 'destroyers' to extend the attacks on
symbols of apartheid. He selected the members by observing the

actions of others in times of public violence. He took note of people who were not scared of the police, as well as those who showed technical proficiency in making petrol-bombs. After keeping track of them over several months, he approached them one by one, and eventually a group was formed which saw as its mission the destruction of the property of 'puppets of the state' who had escaped the net in more public attacks. He was at pains to tell me that while he had formed the group, he was not its leader. The planning of all operations was entirely subject to consensus.

He described with obvious pride a number of episodes in which the group had attacked various buildings and houses. It was clear that he related to each event as an adventure, that there was a game-like quality in the enterprise. In fact, as he told me about each episode, he became quite childlike in his enthusiasm and animation. The excitement inherent in these adventures was obvious and it was re-echoed every time Ricky told his story, despite the fact that he was arrested for them.

During 1985–88 Ricky was in fact arrested five times. He states that he was tortured twice during this period, an experience he describes as follows:

> I was arrested again in June 1986. I was in solitary [confine-ment] for four months. They came every now and then to interrogate me, but nothing serious happened. Then early one morning they came and fetched me and started asking ques-tions about the people who had left in 1985 for training [as guerillas].
>
> They shocked me. They put a bag over my head which stopped my breathing and they shocked me near my kidneys. I needed a doctor but they just left me in solitary. The next day they did the same thing. I said they should kill me.
>
> They took me outside and gave me a box of matches and put a tyre with petrol in it around my neck. They said, 'Just light it.' They put a bag on my head. They hit me. I could smell the petrol. Then they just put me back in solitary.
>
> I thought I was going mad. I used to worry that I would for-get what I was thinking of. I thought I was mad.

Ricky claims in retrospect that his arrest and experience of torture strengthened rather than broke his spirit. In prison he had the opportunity of meeting others and of sharing experiences with them, which he found to be very supportive.

Reflecting back over the 1984–86 period, he feels that the youth made a number of errors. He believes that there was a lack of thorough organisation and discipline. Not enough time was devoted to bridging gaps with the older generation; this allowed the development of divisions in the community which could then be exploited by conservative elements.

One of the issues which brought these divisions to the fore was the question of a national schools boycott. This was not sufficiently discussed with all the people affected by it, particularly the parents. About half the pupils in the school, aided by pupils from a neighbouring township, had forced their will on the rest of the pupils, disregarding the parents' attitudes.

The lack of proper democratic consultation in these actions led to the failure of the endeavour. It also paved the way for the vigilantes' rise to power. According to Ricky, it was not only the police who helped the vigilantes, but also a very strong *inyanga,* a practitioner of traditional medicine who uses herbs for bewitchment and for curative purposes and who believes in the ways of the ancestors and shades. The idea that the vigilantes were aided by *inyangas* using witchcraft was generally shared in the Wilgespruit group, and they believed that this made effective resistance doubly difficult. In Ricky's view, before the vigilantes, who are still powerful in Leandra, can be defeated, their *inyanga* will have to be sought out and killed.

Ricky experiences no conflict about the disciplined use of violence in the struggle, and supports armed resistance unambiguously. He feels that violence was not used sufficiently in Leandra during 1984–86. The one mistake he believes Chief Mayisa made was saving a man called Joseph from a hostile crowd. Joseph was seen as an outcast in the community because he had shot a woman on the instructions of his white employer during an incident of public violence. Two weeks later, as Joseph was bicycling into Leandra during a work stayaway, he was attacked by the crowd. Mayisa intervened to save his life, arguing that Joseph had killed the woman in error and that 'black-on-black' violence was in any event a self-defeating exercise. Ricky still maintains that Mayisa was wrong in this; had Joseph been severely dealt with, a strong message would have gone out to the community about the importance of solidarity and the price of collaborating with the oppressors.

However, this should not give the impression that Ricky is committed to violence for its own sake. He is not. He sees the use of violence in strategic and functional terms within the context of the legitimacy of armed resistance and the notion of a just war. His disapproval of gratuitous violence is evident in the following description of an event which involved a friend of his; he feels it epitomises the essence of true comradeship to which he aspires.

It occurred in an adjacent township at the height of the conflict. A white welfare worker happened to be there at a moment at which tensions were erupting into violence. A group of youths had stopped her and had wanted to stone her car. The friend intervened, possibly risking his own life given the tension of the moment. He pointed out how indiscriminate their actions were and that the social worker was an ally, one who had a perfectly legitimate reason for being in the township. He then escorted her out through the back roads, once again risking his own safety, as he now had to run the gauntlet of the security forces who had barricaded the exits.

Ricky cites this episode as one characteristic of the true comrade who will risk everything for his or her principles. For Ricky, this risk involves being prepared both to kill and to die for these values. He stresses the need always to have one's principles foremost in one's mind and to evaluate and assess the worth of a proposed course of action within these terms. He is totally against actions which are informed not by values but personal motives of revenge or gain.

He believes that motives of personal revenge are most destructive. His dilemma at present is how to bring about a rapprochement between many former vigilantes who regret their earlier alignments and the comrades. The bane of his life is those comrades who will not forgive such vigilantes because of feelings of personal aggrievement, distrust and a desire for revenge. He is impatient with these personal considerations which block progress in confronting the real issues. He is aware that in expressing his impatience he may antagonise some of the comrades and that he may be putting himself at risk. Nevertheless, he feels compelled to do so.

Ricky is, however, a skilled negotiator and he has a subtle appreciation of how far it is possible to push a point at any given moment. He has the ability to strike the right chord in his listeners. He is aided in this by his strong conviction that discussion and negotiation are vital aspects of the process of liberation.

Ricky sees himself as a religious person; he goes to church regularly and prays every day. He feels that religion has been a great source of strength and comfort to him. He wishes to train to be a

minister when he leaves school, a role in which he believes he can
be of service to his people. He believes the church is an effective
site of struggle and that it must consolidate itself in support of the
oppressed. He believes the role of the minister is to provide inspira-
tion and comfort on all levels and to help individuals live up to their
ideals. In his stress on the importance of religion in everyday life,
Ricky is similar to Sisi, also a leader, whose case-study follows.

Sisi

At the time of the follow-up interviews Sisi was nineteen years
old. She is solidly built and has a calm, contained presence. She was
quite relaxed during the interviews and gave the impression of
being comfortable with herself and her views. She seemed old
beyond her years. She was warm, and one had the definite feeling
that she could be relied on in a crisis. Like Ricky, she was clearly
seen by others as a resource person. There is a strength about her
and she seems very level-headed and clear-thinking.

Sisi has spent her whole life with her uncle and aunt, her mother's
sister. Her biological parents divorced when she was very young
and her father disappeared. She does not remember him at all. Her
mother worked as a shop assistant; she has had only sporadic contact with her. She clearly regards her uncle and aunt as her primary
caretakers.

Her uncle works for the local airline as a luggage handler. Her
aunt, until recently, worked in a clothing factory. During her childhood she was looked after by a neighbour while her aunt was at
work; her aunt would leave food and everything else she might
need with this neighbour, whom Sisi remembers as being of a
kindly disposition. She reports that her aunt and uncle were strict
but reasonable, and she experienced them as very concerned.

They have four of their own children, all of whom are younger
than Sisi; they all live in a three-bedroomed house. One of the children for whom Sisi takes a great deal of responsibility is only a tod-
dler. Sisi herself is currently two months pregnant. She will not
marry the father of her child and does not anticipate much support
from him, as he is young and unemployed. Nevertheless, she wants
to have the baby and feels positive about the pregnancy.

She loves school and is very popular. Her performance has placed
her in the top quarter of her class. Her schooling was disrupted
when she joined the struggle in 1983 at the age of thirteen. At fourteen she was forced to go on the run because she was wanted by

the police.

The events which precipitated Sisi's flight from Leandra for the first time involved an attack on the house of a city councillor. She described what happened as follows:

> The day after his house was burned the group most heavily involved in this action were informed upon by a young woman of the township called Joy. The township was then raided by the police who arrested the wrong people, but these people on their release tipped us off as to who was informing on us.
>
> A meeting was held which involved about fifty of those who had been involved in the incident, and it was decided that Joy would be confronted. The boys at the meeting decided that the girls should handle the situation and a group of twenty-four of us women then marched to her house, singing songs and dancing. We were in an angry mood. We surrounded her house. Some of us, myself included, remained outside, while a small group went in to discuss the issues with the family. While we were talking, Joy somehow escaped or perhaps she had left before we arrived, but we knew then that she would have returned to the police.
>
> We were very angry because our intention had been to take her to Mayisa to discipline her. Even though she was an informer we hadn't intended to kill her as this was a first offence. She needed to be given a big fright. She needed to have issues explained to her so she could understand what we were fighting for, but she escaped. In fact, she ran away from Leandra altogether and she only returned in 1988.
>
> She had done us a lot of damage. We knew then that she would definitely give the police a complete list of people and we would all be arrested. So I fled from Leandra and stayed away with my cousins in Bethal until it was safe to return in 1985.

At the beginning of 1986 Sisi, who was then sixteen, had once again to leave Leandra. This time it was the vigilantes rather than the police who were the cause of her flight. When she left Wilgespruit and returned to Leandra in mid-1986, she was one of the group most severely harassed by the vigilantes. Her uncle therefore sent her to school in Germiston where she remained for one year, at which point her aunt had a stroke and Sisi left school to take care of her and the rest of the family. She has now completed eight years of schooling which is more than the majority of the black population achieve.

In reflecting upon her participation in the struggle, Sisi believes that what helped her become involved was the degree to which her home was politicised. Her aunt belonged to a trade union and was active in it. Her uncle was not a union member as his workforce was not unionised, but he was sympathetic both to her involvement and that of her aunt. Sisi also had numerous cousins who visited from Soweto and Bethal and left her informed of events in other townships. She found this contact particularly useful, as she felt it gave her a broad perspective and placed the problems in Leandra in a nation-wide context. She developed a sense of solidarity with black people throughout the country, a sense that was reinforced when she went on the run in 1984.

Sisi's aspirations for her future include full-time involvement as a community organiser. She has joined the Young Christian Students and believes that this group is still making a contribution at local level. She sees the major difficulty in Leandra in 1989 as the great degree of mistrust that exists between members of the community; she feels that an enormous amount of work needs to be done to build trust and bring about unity.

She supported community participation in the 1988 local elections, as she feels that having sympathetic community councillors would be less divisive. She believes that fostering unity is essential; this can be achieved by mobilising the community to pressurise the powers-that-be about local issues which affect everyone, and where gains are potentially possible.

She believes the most important attributes of a comrade are loyalty, courage and flexibility. She stresses the last-mentioned as one that distinguishes a true comrade from one who is simply involved in the struggle for 'his own enjoyment'. Sisi believes true comrades should be able to use a variety of strategies to gain their objectives and should not rely solely on demonstrations and public violence. In her view many, if not most, of the comrades involved in the struggle of 1984–86 were simply swept up in events, without really thinking through what they were doing.

Sisi refers to this type of comrade as follows:

> They joined for their own enjoyment – not really out of real understanding of the issues and certainly not to work. They

were attracted by the slogans and the songs. They enjoyed the toyi-toyi and the singing and throwing stones and the running away from the police. They liked action and were not really keen on spending hours in meetings listening to the problems of the community and strategising how best to approach them.

She feels that because most comrades joined for the action they did not have staying power. This is why they are no longer involved, now that the struggle has moved into a different phase, one which requires a lower profile and a different kind of work.

She is in favour of the use of violence, provided that it has a purpose and is used instrumentally, that it sends out a message to the community. She is unequivocal in her support of attacks on hard targets like government installations, military and police. She has more difficulty in contemplating attacks on soft targets such as shopping centres and restaurants. It bothers her that innocent people may be killed in such situations. However, she says that in certain circumstances this may be justified, as the pain of this will be brief compared to the potential advantages of making the government in particular and whites in general aware of the urgent need for change.

Sisi is philosophical about death: 'It comes to everyone. We will all die and it is better to die for a purpose, achieving something, than to die as a useless thing.' However, she stresses that violence must never be gratuitous. It must be aimed at a specific target for a specific purpose.

She believes that in the past not enough care was taken in determining the truth in disciplinary actions. She gives the example of two policemen she knew, who used their positions to feed information back to community leaders. Members of the community who were not well informed were very antagonistic to these men, whom they perceived to be symbols of apartheid. Yet they served a very important function in the struggle. She believes therefore that the complexity of situations needs to be taken into account, requiring hard work and thought, and not impulsive action.

She feels that she herself is sustained in her participation by her family and her religion. Her family are very religious; they pray together almost daily and are regular church-goers. Furthermore, she feels that the church has a vital role to play in the liberation struggle: far more mobilisation needs to take place in this forum.

As we reflect upon Ricky and Sisi it is clear that if Western standards of what constitutes a 'normal' childhood and adolescence are applied, they should certainly be seen as individuals at risk. From birth, both have been subjected to events which, in the psychological literature, have been classified as major stressors of childhood.

Both of them were separated from their biological mothers in the first two years of life. Both sustained some uprooting in the first eight years of life, occasioned by a change of residence. Both were subjected to poverty and poor living conditions. They were exposed to high levels of violence in their communities and to death and illness in their own families, and all of this occurred prior to their mid-teens.

Specific stressors for Ricky were the death of his father when he was fourteen years old, and having to flee the township when he was sixteen. By this time he had been detained twice. A specific stressor for Sisi was having to flee the township when she was fourteen years old and again when she was sixteen.

Sisi was detained at the time of the Wilgespruit arrests, but unlike Ricky she has never been tortured. Ricky was first detained and tortured at the age of fifteen years, and detained again at the ages of sixteen and seventeen. Thus by the age of nineteen, at the time of follow-up, both Sisi and Ricky had been exposed to what would be considered to be major multiple stressors in the psychological literature. Yet by all standards they both functioned extremely well as individuals. Neither Ricky nor Sisi showed any gross signs of physical or psychological disturbance. There were no signs of clinical depression or excessive anxiety. Neither complained of sleep disturbances, mood fluctuations, physical ailments or any other symptoms. They both presented as cheerful, animated adolescents who were vigorously and constructively engaged with life.

Both Ricky and Sisi have achieved more in their school careers than would be normal for their peers. Only 40 per cent of children in black schools complete more than seven years of schooling (*Daily News*, 3 April 1991). They have positive relationships with their friends and peers and show high levels of empathy and pro-social behaviour. Sisi talks of her aunt's illness with great feeling and sees it as her duty to care for her. She regrets having to leave school but shows no resentment or anger in relation to her aunt and uncle, in this regard. Similarly, Ricky shows a great deal of emotional concern and commitment when he speaks about his family and most particularly his mother, with whom he clearly feels a very close bond.

The only feature in Ricky's and Sisi's lives that would perhaps be questioned is their early parenthood. However, this needs to be seen in context, as both single and young parenthood are not infrequent occurrences in the black urban community. Furthermore, during 1984–86, in many townships there was considerable peer group pressure on young people to produce children for the revolution, a pressure which has symbolic significance. Population control among blacks has long been promoted by the government, which has established free family-planning clinics and spends a great deal of money on propaganda encouraging blacks, but not whites, to limit their families. The encouragement of reproduction was therefore seen as an act of defiance.

In this context both Sisi and Ricky feel positive about their early parenthood, which bodes well for their adjustment to parenthood. They have maintained very positive relationships with their families of origin, which have accepted their situation. They are well integrated into their families and take their fair share of responsibility within them.

The pro-social behaviour Ricky and Sisi show in regard to their families extends to their communities. Both are seen by other group members as resource individuals. Thus by a variety of criteria, including scholastic achievement, social–emotional functioning and pro-social behaviour, Ricky and Sisi represent strongly functioning individuals in their particular communities. Yet considering that both their backgrounds encompass events which would be labelled major stressors in the psychological literature, one would expect the opposite to obtain.

There is a large body of traditional literature which traces adult psychopathology to trauma in childhood. This literature would predict that Ricky and Sisi are at risk for later psychopathology. However, in recent times this traditional view has been challenged by work on both 'normal' adults and children. The practice of assuming that certain hardships and trauma are automatically pathogenic has been heavily criticised. Far greater emphasis is now being placed on factors which may mediate the impact of stressors on the individual. It is increasingly recognised that adverse circumstances are not experienced as equally stressful by all individuals, in all circumstances, all of the time. The actual experience of stress is dependent on the individual's assessment of the seriousness of a particular situation, as well as his or her assessment of resources available to facilitate coping with it. There is an increasing focus therefore on factors which encourage resilience. With this development in mind, the backgrounds of Sisi and Ricky bear further examination to elucidate what might have facilitated their high levels of resilience.

All the youth in the Leandra group could be considered to be at risk for psychological disturbance within the purview of the traditional literature. All their lives had encompassed multiple hardships, including poverty, overcrowding and poor schooling. They had also all been subjected to multiple trauma in their later lives, as this study has documented. It was not surprising, therefore, that at the time the counsellors were called in, in the immediate aftermath of the violence in Leandra and the police raid at the Wilgespruit centre, almost everyone showed signs of psychological disturbance. This took the form of sleep disturbances, psychosomatic symptoms, posttraumatic stress disorder, and so on. Most of the group recovered from these symptoms in a relatively short period. The intrusive thoughts, nightmares and anxiety connected to the events in Leandra and Wilgespruit also abated relatively quickly.

At the time of follow-up, however, a number showed other signs of disturbance. Discussions with key informants, who knew members of the group well, revealed that approximately 20 per cent of the original group were then abusing alcohol or marijuana or both. Abuse was defined as the use of these substances to the degree that functioning in everyday life was impaired on a regular basis for at least two days a week. This criterion was suggested by the key informants themselves. It will be recalled that abuse of marijuana by approximately 5 per cent of the group was already evident at Wilgespruit, but by the time of follow-up it had increased substantially. A further 10 per cent of the group were thought to be involved in gangsterism and petty crime at the time of follow-up, and of these, half were considered to be comtsotsis (youth using the pretext of political activism as a justification for delinquent or criminal activity). Furthermore, in the follow-up interviews, five of the twenty-five subjects interviewed, in other words 20 per cent of this sub-group, showed clear signs of chronic rather than acute posttraumatic stress disorder, psychosomatic symptomatology, depression or anxiety sufficiently severe to interfere with their functioning in life. In conclusion, then, if the above figures are accurate and are extrapolated to the entire group, it would appear that about 50 per cent of the original group at the time of follow-up manifested signs of psychological disturbance.

This incidence figure at first sight seems very high as it means that one in every two persons in the Leandra group at the time of follow-up was not coping in these terms. However, the reciprocal of this is also true: one out of every two persons *was* coping against tremendous odds. Given the extraordinarily high levels of trauma this group sustained in the context of their backgrounds, which already encompassed multiple hardships, it could be argued that this figure is a testimony to the resilience of the human spirit.

Furthermore, individuals like Ricky and Sisi were not only free of symptoms but were functioning at a high level on a number of indices. They were able to work in the broad sense of the term: they were able to harness energy to self-initiated projects, they were able to love, to play, to think well of themselves, to evidence pro-social behaviour, and on the whole maintain a positive sense of well-being despite the harshness of their environment. That is, they fell into the category of the invulnerables or highly stress-resistant individuals (Anthony & Cohler, 1987). Such individuals are de-scribed in the literature as persons who not only cope with multiple stressors, but who may even perform better under adversity. They overcome adversity and use it to increase their range of skills.

The descriptions in the literature of these stress-resistant individ-uals are congruent with those of the consistent leaders in this study. They are described as being directed outward, curious about their environments, and having a range of competencies which they actively develop. Certainly both Ricky and Sisi had these attributes.

Ricky's constant attempt to read my motives and to understand how I operated in the world was part of his outward-directedness and curiosity. Sisi, too, in her thirst for knowledge from her visiting cousins and relatives, showed an outward orientation toward the world as well as a healthy curiosity. Furthermore, that both Ricky and Sisi had a range of competencies was illustrated by their perfor-mance in a number of areas.

Like the true invulnerables described by Anthony (1987), Ricky and Sisi were able to represent outer reality authentically and clearly, and to be pro-active within it, without being impulsive. Both of them thought carefully about their actions and assessed what would be appropriate in the face of the particular reality that con-fronted them. They were both interpersonally skilful and popular. They appraised themselves positively and had a sense of personal responsibility for their own actions and the well-being of others. All these characteristics have been found in the child development literature to be highly correlated with stress resistance and invulnerability. They also showed an ability to make sense of their worlds, to relate meaningfully to them, and to operate in a way which allowed them to manage their worlds by, for example, focusing on what they could change rather than what they could not.

In considering the Leandra youth, literature which pertains to children, adolescents and young adults is all relevant. At Wilgespruit there were fourteen youths aged 12–15 years, thirty-four aged 16–18, and twelve over the age of 18. At the time of follow-up, the median age was 19. In examining the issue of the resilience of the group, the literature pertaining to childhood is particularly important, as it examines factors in early life which seem to foster resistance in the face of adversity. A triad of factors has been shown by numerous researchers to be associated with resilience. This encompasses constitutional factors, the presence of supportive family networks, and an external social support system (Garmezy, 1983). Of all the constitutional factors, age has been the factor most consistently examined in studies on resilience. This is not because increasing age is thought either to confer resilience or to undermine it; the importance of age lies rather in the fact that the impact of any stressor is crucially dependent on the structural readiness of an organism to cope with it (Kagan, 1983). For example, children are generally considered to be more vulnerable than adolescents or adults in terms of their dependence on environmental supports and structures in times of crisis. However, this vulnerability is often offset by children's cognitive limitations and lowered expectations from the environment. These lowered expectations concerning their ability to cope allow the child not to feel responsible for coping, and hence to feel less humiliated for failing to do so. Their cognitive limitations often mean they cannot fully understand the implications of dangerous events, and this moderates their impact.

Both the nature of the events that are experienced as stressful and the mechanisms that are used to cope with them change over time. There are particular periods during which specific events will be experienced in a more stressful way than at others. Separation from one's primary caretakers, for example, has been shown to be maximally stressful between the ages of six months and four years (Rutter, 1981). Below six months, infants have not yet really formed selective attachments. Above four years, children are better able to understand time, and thus have a better appreciation that people continue to exist in their absence.

Sisi and Ricky both sustained early separations. Ricky's separation occurred in the period deemed by Rutter to be critical, while Sisi's did not. She was separated from her mother and placed with her aunt at about three months. Ricky on the other hand was separated from his mother and left in the care of his grandmother when he was about two years old. He knew his grandmother well, however, as he had often spent evenings and weekends with her prior to his placement.

Although Sisi sustained no further long-term separations from her primary caretaker during childhood, her aunt went out to work when she was only two years old, leaving her in the care of a neighbour. Once again, Sisi was familiar with the neighbour; she remembers her as kind, and believes that her aunt left everything with the neighbour that she might have needed.

How satisfactory this arrangement was in reality is impossible to tell. Similarly, it is impossible in retrospect to determine what reaction both Sisi and Ricky had at the time to their separation from their primary caretakers. They may well have shown reactions of distress. Indeed, it would be surprising if they had not. It is only possible to say at this point that the separations had no enduring damaging effects and that both Ricky and Sisi currently reconstruct these events in positive terms.

The positive reconstruction of events is in itself linked to invulnerability and stress resistance (Antonovsky, 1987). The root of this kind of optimism is believed to be linked both to the environment and to certain constitutional factors. These constitutional factors, which can be observed in the first few days of life, include the capacity for a rapid decline of autonomic nervous system activity after frustration or stress, and an active engagement with the world, including the infant's acting upon the world and the ability to elicit a response from it. A further favourable temperamental factor is a pattern of eating and sleeping that is rhythmic (Murphy, 1987).

Returning to Ricky and Sisi, we cannot in retrospect establish the original basic temperaments of our protagonists. Suffice it to say that both are currently very charming and engaging persons to whom it is difficult not to respond. Both are described retrospectively by their caretakers as being easy babies who had no sleeping or eating difficulties. The accuracy of this recall is impossible to establish, as is the degree to which it may be influenced by current perceptions. Nevertheless, the indications are that both Ricky and Sisi were temperamentally easy to begin with, which partly explains their later resistance to adverse circumstances.

The leaders were not the only resilient members of the Leandra group, however. Many of the followers were similarly resistant to stress, even though at the time of follow-up they were not in leadership positions. An examination of the case vignettes of a number of the followers will therefore be undertaken to establish factors in their backgrounds which may have facilitated their stress resistance, and also to ascertain if there were factors which perhaps differentiated between the leaders and the followers.

THE FOLLOWERS

The followers comprised a diverse and heterogeneous group. Individuals were included in this classification by exclusion from the other categories of leader, comtsotsi or victim. The followers were those who were not in leadership positions at the time of follow-up, although a few may have been leaders at Wilgespruit. They were not anti-social and they were also not sufficiently dysfunctional to be called victims or casualties. Some of the followers were heroes in search of a script, some were simply conformists, others again seemed to use the struggle as a conduit for the expression of their own emotions, allowing themselves in turn to be used by it.

It must be stressed again, however, that all these categories were very fluid and permeable. Today's follower could well become tomorrow's leader, as will be seen in the case of Isaac who typifies the group I have identified as heroes in search of a script. Similarly, mounting pressures may well push a functioning individual over the boundary into dysfunction, as will be clear in the case of Nicholas, who typified the sub-group termed the lightning-conductors or conduits. Finally, even conformists like Pretty might in certain circumstances, in an impulsive moment, perform acts of heroism or altruism which could be transformative. Human beings remain infinitely complex even when they are caught up in powerful historical processes. Their individual life histories are certainly shaped by these historical processes, but the unique life history of an individual will influence the particular form his or her involvement in these processes will take. This will become clear when prototypic forms of involvement in the struggle are considered.

Heroes in Search of a Script

This group seemed to enter the struggle as a way of giving meaning and direction to their lives. They romanticised their participation and identified strongly with the image of what Jay Lifton (1973) has called the warrior-hero. According to Lifton, the warrior-hero is a figure understood and celebrated by almost all known cultures. He dedicates his life to the collective good, working to improve the lot of his people. He enhances not only their material position, but also their spiritual wisdom: in other words, he works to expand their consciousness.

Campbell (1956) describes the warrior-hero as the champion of things to come: 'the dragon to be slain by him is precisely the monster of the status quo.... the enemy is great and conspicuous in the seat of power; he is the enemy, the dragon tyrant because he turns to his own advantage the authority of this position. The mythical hero ... brings a knowledge of the secret of the tyrant's doom. The deeds of the warrior-hero increase a people's sense of its immortal cultural and racial substance' (in Lifton, 1973, p. 26). On an individual level, the warrior-hero encompasses courage, loyalty, honour and technical proficiency. These qualities are all channelled into the service of the love the warrior-hero bears for his people, and he will not only risk death himself but also kill in the service of this love. Such killing, however, is never gratuitous, being linked with the symbolism of regeneration. The warrior-hero is permitted to kill but not to destroy life. He is permitted to kill only to enlarge and perpetuate life (Campbell, 1956).

One difference between the consistent leaders and the heroes in search of a script lay in the degree to which each internalised this image and made it his or her own. The leaders had already integrated the image into their identities. It was a part of who they were. They were no longer experimenting with and trying to play the role of the warrior-hero; they *were* warrior-heroes, and had taken on the personal responsibility that this implies. They brought their independence of thought and insight to bear on their experience, and took on the burden and the consequences of communicating their resolution. Ricky was prepared to express his disagreement with Chief Mayisa's approach to Joseph; he was similarly able to voice the unpopular notion that the vigilantes should be forgiven and reintegrated into the community. Sisi similarly evidenced an ability to express independent views.

The leaders' participation in the struggle seemed to be guided by an identity that was already formed and had some coherence. Obviously participation reinforced this, but they were not using the struggle to give coherence to their identity; their participation was an expression of this coherence. In this sense they were at a different developmental level from the heroes in search of a script, who still needed the image of the warrior-hero as something external to themselves to play into. The heroes in search of a script also desired to be controlled and directed by an idealised authority figure. They found security and comfort in this, a refuge from the ambiguities of the outer world and the complexities of their inner worlds, as the following vignette of Isaac illustrates.

Isaac

Isaac was born in 1972. He was only thirteen at the time of the crisis in Leandra, and at follow-up was sixteen years old, about three years younger than most of the other informants.

He is a well-built, good-looking young man. Like Ricky, he has charm, but conveys an impression of vulnerability. He likes to project an image of himself as a soldier and a warrior-hero, and in some sense this image also reflects the reality of who he is. On another level, however, he is also a young boy who is in need of the comforts of home and a family. This too comes across during interviews. Isaac feels very threatened by this side of himself and whenever it emerges, for instance when he speaks of his loneliness and pain, he retreats from it and takes refuge in bravado.

At such times he appears as a young boy trying to be very manly. When he describes some of his exploits during the riots, there is a sense of excitement in being caught up in these historic events; there seems to be a thin dividing line between macho fantasies and reality. Yet underneath this tough image he likes to present, one has glimpses both of his real empathy for others and of his own vulnerability.

Isaac comes across as a very deep person. There is a complexity about him which is reflected in a preparedness to struggle with ideas, thoughts and feelings. This reflective side of himself is in conflict with his desire for action and involvement as well as his need for group belonging and acceptance. These latter needs are very strong as is appropriate for his age. To fulfil them Isaac is compliant, but this compliance does not blunt his independence of thought nor his own internal struggle with the processes of which he is a part.

He comes from a family of nine siblings. They live in a two-bed-roomed house; he complains of the level of overcrowding. When visitors come, many of the children have to sleep in the dining-room and others in the kitchen. Even when there are no visitors, the dining-room doubles as a bedroom.

Despite the overcrowding and poverty, Isaac reports that his home life was happy. His father, a deacon in the church, always took a great interest in all his children. He helped Isaac with his homework and was always concerned about his scholastic progress, seeing it as the key to his future well-being.

His mother stayed at home to care for the children. Isaac remembers her as very warm. During the school holidays she would buy him new school uniforms and presents because he had passed at school. He was happy there and had never failed a standard.

The family was very cohesive. They attended church regularly and prayed together every night. Since his father's death when he was fourteen years old, Isaac and his brother regularly help to organise prayer services, both on Sundays and during the week.

Neither Isaac's parents nor his grandparents were actively involved in the struggle. However, Isaac's older brother was very active. He disappeared in 1986 and the family have been unable to trace him. The last the family heard of him was that during a period of unrest he was arrested at a roadblock while transporting to hospital a child who had been run over. The family made enquiries at jails and police stations but were never able to establish what had happened. Isaac himself is not sure what he believes. He fluctuates between the view that perhaps his brother escaped and skipped the country to be trained outside, and that he was killed in police custody.

His brother was certainly very active in school politics and was forced to leave school in 1986 after a confrontation with one of the teachers. He was detained shortly after this, accused of being subversive and of persuading others to join popular organisations and to participate in boycotts. He remained in detention for several months.

Isaac believes that his parents were supportive of his brother's participation in the struggle. They were not active themselves but, says Isaac, 'They know that we are slaves. They know that even small children can call adults and old people kaffirs.' He recalls that when he was eleven years old, standing outside a supermarket, a white child of about six or seven came past and called him a kaffir. He gave the boy a slap and the child ran off to tell his father.

Believing that the father would beat him up and that he would have no recourse to any justice, Isaac took flight. He has never forgotten the humiliation of this incident; it was one of the factors which promoted his active participation in the events of 1984–86.

A further factor was the behaviour of the police. He recalls their disrupting local community meetings with teargas and arresting many people for no reason that he could fathom. He believed most of the arrests were arbitrary and that if he were to be arrested, he should at least have been given some cause.

Isaac does not conceive of himself as a leader. He prefers to see himself as a soldier. He describes his role in the following terms: 'I believe in fighting and fighting until we are free. Even if I die I feel it will be worthwhile if I have achieved something before then that will benefit those who remain behind. I get the strength to believe this and keep going from being with many other comrades who feel the same way.'

Isaac longs for the heady days of 1984–86. He feels that at least during this time blacks were proving that they were not cowards. The community was more united in common action and there were more tangible proofs that change could occur. He pays lip-service to the idea of negotiations but at the end of the day he has little faith in the process as he feels that his 'forefathers tried talking for decades, but achieved nothing'.

Isaac's militant stance and his desire for action coexist with a clear mind and a great deal of independent thought. In regard to the group's sojourn at Wilgespruit, for example, he believes that despite the crisis in the township, to leave it was a mistake. In his view it would have been better if the youth had stayed home and tried to work out their differences with the vigilantes through meetings and discussions. During the absence of the comrades, the vigilantes gained too much power in the community. This laid the ground for continued conflict and dissension, which in turn paved the way for co-option of the vigilantes by the state. Isaac believes that it was the comrades' failure to integrate the vigilantes within the struggle after these divisions had occurred which precipitated their joining the municipal police, the 'green beans'. This worsened the situation for the comrades and the community in general, as the 'green beans' could now intimidate the community with greater impunity.

Isaac's independence of thought is revealed further in his attitude to the food boycotts at Wilgespruit. He saw the boycott as very unhelpful as 'these people were really helping us when we had no alternative. They were not the people we were fighting yet we argued with them.' At the time of the boycott Isaac felt unfree to voice his views. He simply joined in because 'the person who started it was our leader, but according to me that boycott was not necessary.'

One of the points that he kept returning to in different ways was the need to distinguish clearly those who were the enemy. For example, he was against necklacing not only because it was 'gruesome' but because it was done to fellow blacks who were not ultimately the enemy. 'The whites don't do this to each other and in the long run it will not work for us either. Even if people are sell-outs they must be harshly disciplined and helped back into the community, not killed. This only increases our problems.'

Isaac claims to have witnessed a necklacing in a neighbouring township. The group had been attending a night vigil for an activist who had died. During the vigil the police intervened with dogs and sjamboks and a number of people were badly beaten up. The following day, during the funeral, a person believed to be a policeman in plain clothes was spotted in the crowd. He was then necklaced.

At the time of the event, Isaac felt that the victim deserved his fate, because the previous evening he had allowed people to be assaulted. 'It was in revenge for this that he was killed and in the moment I felt it was right. When I was alone I felt very bad about it. It was gruesome and it will not really help us. He should have been sjambokked and warned, not necklaced.' Isaac feels similarly about a person dealt with by the comrades:

> I was present when he was punished. The comrades beat him up with anything they came across. He was even stabbed. He was beaten up so badly that he had to be taken to hospital. I still feel bad about it and wish I had the strength to stop them. It is very sad that we are attacking each other like this. We must identify the real enemy and be disciplined in our approach.

When asked if he makes his views known now, Isaac says he does do so, but not vociferously; one has to be cautious about going against the majority view for fear of being labelled oneself. Besides which, he does not feel very comfortable as a public speaker. He feels that his talents lie not in his organisational and planning ability but in his courage. He feels more comfortable in action and is happy to follow instructions, even when he disagrees with them, as he sees unity and cohesion as the most essential factors in the struggle.

Isaac finds the present situation very distressing as nobody, since the rise of the vigilantes, trusts anybody else. He belongs to the Young Christian Students and is very active in it. He also belongs to a soccer club in which political discussions and meetings are frequently held. He is not active at the school level as he has been forced to drop out; since his father's death, the family cannot afford the school fees.

Isaac's future at this point is uncertain. If he succeeds in finding employment, it seems certain that his participation in resistance will continue through the trade-union movement. His commitment is unquestionable, as is his preparedness to make sacrifices for his beliefs. He has proved himself to be resilient and resourceful, and doubtless will make every attempt to take control of his own life. How successful he will be in view of the odds, and what will happen if he fails, remain to be seen. In my view, Isaac shows a great deal of leadership potential. Whether or not he will choose to express it, or be given an opportunity to do so, remains a moot point.

At the moment Isaac is not showing any signs of cracking, even under the strain of unemployment. However, he still has hope that his efforts to find employment will be successful. In the meantime he has found constructive ways to channel his energy through music and sport. Fate and circumstance will have a strong hand in determining his future path.

The complexity and ambiguity in Isaac's perceptions require further comment. It is an ambiguity and complexity of which he is consciously aware. He knows that his responses to the food boycott and the punishment of Joseph, for example, were not uncomplicated. On the whole he chooses to deal with these ambiguities by not entering them too deeply. He finds refuge in his role as a follower, taking comfort in the mode of action rather than of reflection. However, he makes this choice consciously and in this regard he is different from Pretty, the prototype of a conformer, who will be discussed below. Isaac seems much more aware of the range of options open to him than do those who fall into the conformer category. He has chosen from these options a role in which he feels comfortable and which he feels fits the identity he already has. Doubtless this choice will have implications for the consolidation of further development of his sense of self in the world. If one contrasts Isaac's participation in the struggle with that of the conformists, it will become clear that it serves a far more central role in defining his self-image than theirs does.

Viewed against his background Isaac was not emotionally disadvantaged. His warm and cohesive family relations created an environment of emotional safety which underpinned his ability to relate to ambiguity and complexity. He did not experience his immediate environment as dangerous and threatening and thus did not need to reduce his thinking to a categorical level with simplistic divisions of people and events into friends or foes, good or bad. He is capable of, and frequently evidenced, a complexity and subtlety of thought which his home environment made possible. Although Isaac frequently chooses in the present to deal with his complex world by simplifying it, this is a conscious strategy that allows him the freedom to experiment with particular ways of being in the world, which he feels are congruent with his current sense of self and which meet certain central needs. Isaac expresses the common adolescent need to leave an imprint on the world, to be active, and to be altruistic. He is the prototypical adolescent hero in search of a script. The opportunity to participate in a liberation struggle, so patently on the side of justice, provides this script.

The ideals that this struggle encompasses, as well as the notion of the warrior-hero, resonate not only with how Isaac sees himself, but with how the majority of youth in the struggle of 1984–86 saw themselves. There was a general feeling that they were not only responsible for fighting to liberate themselves and their communities, but that they were the bearers of enlightenment to the older generation. They believed that the older generation had capitulated too easily to oppression, partly through ignorance, and partly through fear. That this view was representative is witnessed in the following quote (Lambert & Webster, 1989):

> Our parents still have that old image they grew up under.
> They tell us that the white man is a white man and what he
> says is final.... We are caught in a trap. What our parents don't
> seem to have is a desire for us to be better people.... So now
> we do everything for ourselves without consulting our parents
> because it is useless to talk to a stone.

The ideal of the warrior-hero is a very romantic one, but it nevertheless has the potential to be constructive. It provides positive ideals for adolescents who may use it to consolidate their identities in a pro-social fashion. Potentially, however, it can also be a very dangerous ideal to encourage youth to act into. Because it is romantic and unrealistic, it can promote dangerous, reckless and unstrategic behaviours in relation to those defined as the enemy. Community leaders interviewed at the time are well aware of this and have expressed anxieties in this regard, such as, 'Our youth are brave and they are angry. But stones cannot stop Casspirs.'

The ranks of the youth who act out their frustration often in unstrategic and reckless ways are swelled not only by the heroes in search of scripts, but by the conformists and lightning-conductors (or conduits) alike.

The Conduits

This set of followers is paradoxical in that they often present as leaders. This is particularly true in moments of heightened emotionality in the group, during which these individuals gain prominence as they have an uncanny ability to articulate and express the sentiments of the group. They are highly intuitive and responsive to the collective mood and act in conformity with it. They are, however, not true leaders because their primary mode of living is reactive rather than proactive. Unlike true leaders, they will not intervene when appropriate to persuade the group to alter the course upon which it has embarked. They act rather to amplify and exaggerate group sentiments; in this sense they act as conduits.

Just as the conduits give expression to the moods of the group, so too do they use it as a vehicle for the discharge of their own emotions. They lack a clearly defined sense of self and use the group in their search for definition. In this sense they are different from the heroes in search of a script, who may also discharge emotions in the group, but who are not dependent on it for their primary identity in the way the conduits are. The heroes in search of a script are far more preoccupied than the conduits with developing and living into an ego ideal or image of themselves that they find acceptable. The conduits are not sufficiently differentiated as personalities to be focused on living into a self-defined ideal. They are still struggling with raw emotions and are caught in a symbiotic relationship with the corporate body. However, their ability to perceive the needs, moods and sentiments of others, both on an individual and on a group level, is remarkable and may at times of heightened emotionality lead to their being thrust into leadership positions, as in the case-study that follows.

Nicholas

Nicholas was twenty years old at the time of follow-up. He was seventeen when he fled Leandra. He is tall and pleasant-looking. An air of anxiety and nervousness emanates from him. He is unrelaxed and intertwines his fingers and separates them continuously. He makes intermittent eye contact and seems preoccupied and withdrawn. He becomes particularly anxious when he speaks of his fears that he will be banned from school next year. He is currently in Standard eight but has been labelled an activist, and it was only through the influence of a relative that he was allowed into school at all. Apart from this label, he is over eighteen years old, which makes it more difficult in terms of current school regulations for him to remain a pupil.

He is one of six siblings, the third child; he has two older and two younger sisters, and a brother. His parents still live together, although there is a great deal of family conflict occasioned by his father's drinking. His father, who is employed at an oil refinery as a semi-skilled worker, resides at his site of employment and only returns on weekends.

Nicholas feels that as a child he was closer to his father than to his mother. He used to look forward to his coming home over the weekend, despite the fact that he sporadically abused alcohol and, when he did so, made life extremely difficult for the family.

Nicholas recalls the following episode particularly clearly. He was fighting with his sister. His father was sitting outside drinking. Suddenly he appeared at the door and descended upon them. They fled and hid in a cupboard in the bedroom. His father pursued them and threatened to burn the cupboard down. His mother intervened and there was a violent fight. He, his mother and siblings fled and spent the night with his aunt until his father cooled down. This was the worst episode of alcohol-related violence that he recalls. It was not, however, the only one involving family violence. Nevertheless, he remembers his father, when not drunk, as someone he could talk to and with whom he could share his problems. In this, he comments, his father was unlike his mother. He was also different from his mother in that when he was not drunk he was not punitive. Nicholas's main concern about his father's drinking was the disgrace he brought on the family. Nicholas is very aware of and sensitive to social opinion and censure, and when he speaks of this disgrace he becomes even more withdrawn and looks at the floor.

He does not remember his mother as a warm person. He experienced her as very punitive, as the following incident illustrates. It occurred on the way to school when Nicholas was about eight years old. He did not want to go to school on that particular day and was dawdling and scuffing his shoes. His mother first grew impatient and then infuriated and started to give him a hiding. She was not wearing a belt and so she stopped and asked a man walking down the road to lend her his. Nicholas experienced this as very humiliating; the man who obliged laughed at him, adding insult to injury.

Nicholas's unhappy memories of his family life are, to some extent, offset by other happier childhood memories. For example, he and his sisters and a group of neighbourhood children would often swim in a dam owned by a white school principal who was away from home in the mornings. This gave them plenty of time to play before he returned. Sometimes they would forget the time and he would find them there. Then they had to run as fast as their legs could carry them, usually escaping triumphantly.

The older children in the swimming group were also looked after by the woman his mother paid to care for him and his sisters. His memories of this caretaker are generally kindly but there were times when she did not give them the food their mother had left for them. She would give them inferior food and keep theirs for herself. Yet he believes she was warm and caring, and on the whole he felt comfortable with her.

He joined the struggle in 1983. He was persuaded by an older friend; this friend introduced him to Abel Nkabinde, a community leader whom he admired. Nicholas had been involved in organisations for some time before the events that erupted between 1984 and 1986, not in a leadership role, but as part of a larger disciplinary committee, the members of which were by and large older than he was. At this time in Leandra, as in many other townships, an anti-crime campaign had been organised by local residents. People set up their own committees and courts to hear complaints about thefts, assaults and community conflicts of various kinds, including marital conflicts and disputes between neighbours. These courts would hear the complaints, pass judgment and determine punishments, which would often involve the guilty party being sjambokked for his or her misdeeds.

There were two groups involved in the disciplinary committee:

those who were primarily responsible for hearing the complaints and deciding upon the outcome, and those responsible for punishment. Nicholas was part of the latter group. A further function of the disciplinary committee was that of primary crime prevention. Attempts were made to clean up the streets. Drunkenness was particularly frowned upon and individuals who were found on the streets drunk, especially if they were behaving aggressively or carrying a weapon, were apprehended and the weapon was confiscated.

The establishment of disciplinary committees and people's courts evoked strong reaction from the state, and individuals associated with them were open to charges of attempted subversion. The communities themselves received these committees with mixed feelings. At first their attitudes were positive, as they did succeed in inhibiting crime. However, the committees tended to overstep the mark and exceed the boundaries of what the community perceived to be legitimate activities geared toward crime prevention. Considering the youth of many of those on the committees, there was particular resentment at their involvement in, for example, marital conflicts. There were also occasions when members of the committees were suspected of abusing this structure to settle personal scores.

During my interview with Nicholas, he commented at length on the advantages and disadvantages of the disciplinary committees, as he saw them. He is in favour of their re-establishment, given their effectiveness in crime prevention. However, he acknowledges the errors of the past and sees the need for members of these committees to exercise more restraint in the future.

In reflecting on his past, Nicholas commented on the degree to which his initial involvement in the struggle and his continued participation in it were inspired by his female friends. In acknowledging this he was unusual. Very few of the young men and boys who were interviewed believed they had been influenced by their female peers despite the fact that a number of women occupied leadership positions during this period. Nicholas, on the other hand, believes that he drew strength from his women friends. He needed this support to cope with his parents, both of whom did not look kindly on his activities. They were, and still are, resistant to his involvement, even at the level of his attending funerals or meetings. He complains that his parents try to prevent him from participating in these activities as they fear for him, but their resistance has made his life very difficult.

In addition to several close friendships with women, Nicholas has been in a stable intimate relationship for the last five years. He describes his partner as a warm, strong person who is respected by others. As yet they have no children, which on one level seems a source of concern, but in view of his financial position he is also relieved.

In general, Nicholas feels despondent about both his own personal future and that of the country. There are signs of an incipient depression. It seems that he is currently being held together and helped to function by the structure and routine of his school life and by his relationship with Daphne. He is managing to cope at the present time with this support, but he seems very fragile and vulnerable.

In reflecting upon Nicholas, we may draw once again certain connections between his early and current life. His earliest memories reflect his interactions with his siblings and peers: most of Nicholas's early caretaking took place in the context of a peer group.

Sibling and peer caretaking is not an unusual style of child-rearing, found in South Africa as well as elsewhere in Africa. A number of the youth in the Leandra group were cared for by older siblings. As they got older these youth in their turn would care for their younger siblings. Most studies on the effects of this form of caretaking on children have been carried out by anthropologists rather than psychologists. One notable exception was a study by Freud and Burlingham (1943), who researched a group of children who had been together in a Nazi concentration camp without consistent adult care. Despite the extremity of their situation, Freud and Burlingham concluded that the children's capacity for trust, care and empathy was not destroyed by their experience. On the contrary, in their interaction with each other they showed very high levels of empathy and concern. For example, they would not go on an outing if one member was missing. If one member of the group was out of the room for too long, both that individual and the entire group became agitated until they were reunited. When some children were given gifts they would demand that others in the group should receive equally. Thus bonding and identification certainly occurred but in a more horizontal peer-group fashion than a vertical parental fashion, as is customary with children of this age in the West.

For those children in the Leandra group whose primary caretakers were siblings or peers, a similar process of horizontal identification with peers, rather than vertical identification with adults, took place.

It was nowhere near as extreme as that reported in the Freud and Burlingham study, because in the Leandra group, parental role models were also available. However, in instances like that of Nicholas where parental relationships were problematic, the sibling and peer groups provided an alternative forum in which trusting, loving, co-operating and caring could be fostered. Nicholas still draws a great deal of sustenance from the peer group, more so than do Ricky, Sisi and Isaac, who are more grounded in the family. It is not only the larger peer group that is important to Nicholas but the intimate friendships he has within these groups.

It is significant that many of Nicholas's important relationships are with women. This seems to reflect his ongoing needs for nurturance and comfort. During my contact with him he was less concerned than many of the other boys with projecting a macho image. He seemed quite comfortable in his male identity and did not feel that his courage was in question or that he needed to prove it. This could be because Nicholas is in fact perceived by others in the group as very courageous.

During interviews with him, he showed a palpable vulnerability which bore a different quality from that of Isaac. Isaac's was somehow related to his age and developmental stage. He was a young boy trying to be a man. Nicholas's vulnerability seemed to be related to a deep-seated yearning for nurturance, belonging and peace of mind. There was a lost quality about him, yet on the surface he was holding himself together and functioning reasonably well.

He has made a good choice in his selection of Daphne as a partner. She is nurturant and caring. His need for intimacy has created fewer problems for him than his need for belonging. His dependence on the peer group for approval has led him into difficulties. He feels pressurised by the peer group and he therefore puts more energy into his involvement in various organisations than he himself feels he can afford. He wishes to escape and to start anew. When asked if he wished to continue at school, he expressed reservations. Were he to continue, he would wish to be in a new school where people did not know him. He wanted to escape the label of activist: he felt persecuted by the authorities because of it, but also under pressure by his peers to maintain this profile.

Nicholas certainly seems to be in need of time out. However, it is doubtful that going to a new school will provide this. His above-average need to be engaged with his peer group and to be actively connected with them, coupled with the lack of alternative family support, will pressurise him into continuing to act as a conduit for the group's moods and wishes. His above-average intelligence, his own sensitivity to the group, and his exceptional ability to mirror its moods accurately will ensure that he always stands out in some way.

Just as Nicholas mirrors the group's moods and desires, there are times when the group also mirrors his own. It is noteworthy that, given his conflict-stricken background and his early and continued exposure to family violence, Nicholas chose and was chosen to serve on the disciplinary committee. In this role he was able, in a socially acceptable manner, to give vent to anger which not only pertained to the injustices of society, but had its roots in his own unfair and abusive treatment within the family. Nicholas openly expressed his satisfaction in serving in this role. He did not feel sorry for those who were whipped. He believed that 'people who do not want to listen must be taught a lesson'. His attitude to this should not be taken out of context. In a recent study on the attitude of ordinary black children to discipline, it was found they favoured harsh discipline for what seemed to be fairly minor infringements even within their family circles (Setiloane, 1990).

This must be seen within the general culture of violence which prevails in ghettos and at the same time within particular beliefs about the family. Many of the youth in the Leandra group similarly favoured vigorous disciplinary measures within the family. Strict discipline was perceived as an indication of concern. They felt that members of a family are bound by that family's rules, which it behoves them to respect. Infringements should be dealt with severely as discipline, even harsh discipline, serves to solidify family bonds. It is not intended to be alienating. In reflecting on their own lives the majority of the group felt that this message concerning family solidarity had been clearly communicated to them when they had been punished for disobedience. They endorsed both the disciplinary actions and the rule-setting of their parents. The only time they felt parental rules should be challenged as a matter of course was when they were aimed at inhibiting participation in the struggle. Such cases should be vigorously opposed as the parents concerned lacked depth of understanding of the issues.

If we return to Nicholas and his experiences with discipline, it seems that these occurred in a more disengaged context than was the case for many of the others in the group. Furthermore, given his father's alcohol abuse, discipline was more likely to be arbitrary than tied to the breaking of clear rules. Nicholas was thus less able to avoid it through his own active endeavours to follow the rules and regulations of the family. This inability to avoid punishment left him angry and resentful. Taking on the role himself of disciplinarian in the struggle allowed him both to express the anger and to grapple with this unresolved issue in some way. In this instance, therefore, there was some fit between the press of internal forces in Nicholas's psyche and the external social issues of the moment. Nicholas could externalise the pain inflicted on him by acting it out in relation to others in a way which was controlled and socially sanctioned rather than in a more random fashion.

This facilitated a split in Nicholas's psyche which allowed the angry and sadistic parts of himself to be encapsulated, leaving his more loving, caring and vulnerable side intact. The existence of a deeply caring part of the self was evident in his relationship with many of the younger members in the group, who confided in him and saw him as a protector. He was obviously seen by Daphne as a warm and caring person, and in his discussion of her, his love and capacity for concern were clear.

Thus Nicholas presented as a very complex, multi-faceted person. There was, however, a certain lack of coherence in his identity which left him dependent on the group for a definition of himself. It also made him more susceptible to acting out and expressing the group sentiment, particularly when this was anger. Discussions, negotiations and involvement in grassroots organisations suit Nicholas's style of being in the world less well than the more overtly active forms of engagement that were the order of the day in 1984–86. Nevertheless, in this area too he has bowed to group pressure. Nicholas is currently active in a number of organisations despite his internal anxiety and depression.

His anxiety and depression are currently aggravated by his developmental stage. At this point in his life he has actively to confront the real life issues of his occupational and personal future. Both look bleak. Nicholas's future, like that of all the others, will ultimately depend on events not only in his personal life, but in the broader environment. His resilience is low, and he is just managing to stave off being overwhelmed by anxiety and depression. He stands poised on the brink of immobilisation. Unlike Matthew who is to be discussed later, Nicholas has not yet crossed the boundary between follower and casualty; however, he is close to it.

The Conformists

The conformists, unlike the heroes in search of a script, are motivated in their concern with liberation more by social conformity than by ideals, or what Rosenhan (1972) termed normative altruism. Although the heroes in search of a script have not yet internalised their ideals and need an image or an external role model to imitate, they are nevertheless primarily motivated by ideals. They are not motivated only by the need to conform to a group, but by a desire to live up to their own image of what they should be. In this they differ from the conformists. The conformists differ again from the conduits in that they are much less symbiotically involved with the group's emotions and moods. The conformists are motivated by group acceptance but their passions are not engaged by the group to the same extent. They also lack the conduits' refined ability to intuit the sentiments of the group. Unlike the conduits, the conformists are seldom thrust into leadership positions at times of heightened emotionality.

Rosenhan (1972) used the term 'normative altruism' to describe the motivation of a particular type of person who participated in the civil rights movement in the USA. They were a group whose participation seemed primarily motivated by short-term personal rewards, approval from the group and the camaraderie generated by the movement at the time. This description certainly fitted a number of people within the Leandra group. An extreme example of such a profile follows.

Pretty

Pretty is eighteen years old. Her mother died when she was thirteen. She lives with the family of her best friend. There are three children in the house, two boys and one girl. Her friend's father works as a motor mechanic; her friend's mother works as a clerk. By Leandra standards they are reasonably affluent. Their house has three bedrooms and is properly furnished and well looked after.

Pretty has been staying with this family for almost five years now, since her mother died of tuberculosis in 1984. She remembers this as very traumatic, not only because she lost her mother, but because she also lost her brother, who went to live with an aunt while she went to live with her friend's family.

Pretty does not remember ever having met her father. Nor does she know where he is. She reports that during her childhood she did not feel excessively deprived because she did not have a father. Many of her friends were in the same boat.

Her mother went back to work when Pretty was two years old. After this she was cared for by her brother. She went to school at the age of eight and is still at school. She enjoys learning but finds her teachers dominating and unsympathetic.

Pretty joined the struggle in 1985, one year after her mother's death, by when she was living with her friend's family. Her involvement came about through people at school who complained about the poor quality of education and the conditions they had to endure. She identified with them, and endorsed their sentiments about the unfairness of increases in rent and food prices which were imposed on the community without explanation or discussion.

What attracted her first was the energy in the group:

> I enjoyed the freedom songs, and the toyi-toyi; they made me feel happy. I joined in when they sang and after that they would usually tell me when they had meetings and I would attend. At that time I did not really understand much about what was happening. I gleaned some information from the meetings. But all the people I spoke to were not well informed, just like me.

Neither her mother nor brother nor the new family she had joined were actively involved in the struggle, but her boyfriend at that time was. He was very guarded about his activities, in which he was careful not to involve Pretty if he thought they could be dangerous. If, for example, he believed that there might be trouble at a meeting, he would forbid her to attend and beat her if she did. Pretty felt positive about this and saw Benjo as protective rather than abusive.

Despite his protectiveness, she did participate in the mass rallies that were held in Leandra, and was present when several of the councillors' houses were stoned and petrol-bombed. Apart from these events in which several hundred youths participated, Pretty was involved in an attack on a small meat lorry driven by a white man. Shortly after sunset, she was walking with her boyfriend and six others near the outskirts of the township when they saw the van, which had broken down. The boys decided after a brief discussion to attack it. Pretty was instructed to wait where she was, out of harm's way but able to observe. The boys armed themselves with stones and surrounded the van. The driver tried to draw a gun but seemed very afraid, and ran away. The boys then broke open the door, and Pretty was called on to help unload and carry away the meat. Afterwards the boys set fire to the van.

Pretty reports that she felt rather scared while she was watching. She was afraid the boys would be shot or that they would subsequently be caught. She felt better when she was actively participating and helping them.

When asked why the boys had attacked the van she indicated that she wasn't very sure. She remembers, though, that they had discussed what the van was doing on the borders of the township and expressed anger at its presence. Their feeling was that they did not have free access to white towns, especially after dark, so why should the white man be in the township? There was a general feeling of anger and resentment about the curfew that had been imposed on some townships at the time and Pretty believes that this partially motivated the attack. She herself felt that this white man, along with most others, was probably exploiting blacks by charging high prices for his meat; this in itself justified the attack.

Pretty was not present at Mayisa's house on the night he was killed. She was, however, present at the funeral. She remembers that it was raining very hard. 'Earlier that day there was no rain, but as soon as we moved to the school for the service, it started raining and there was thunder and lightning. Most people said that when we bury prominent people it is meant to rain that way.'

Pretty says she felt very sad at the funeral of Mayisa because he was a great man and she, as part of the community, mourned his death, although she had never known him personally. She also remembers feeling very afraid at the funeral because of the presence of the vigilantes. Her association with Benjo, her boyfriend, had led to her being labelled an activist as she had been seen at meetings and been involved in boycotts and attacks on councillors' houses.

She was doubly afraid of the vigilantes because she felt that they were practising sorcery and that they had very strong *muthi* or medicine which they had used to bewitch the comrades. She felt this to be true because 'they sent small boys to attack us but we felt afraid and these small boys looked like big men. Even if there were only a few of them, we saw double and it looked as though there were many. This could only have been the *muthi*.'

After the vigilante was killed at Mayisa's funeral, Pretty felt compelled to flee Leandra. She was certain that she would be targeted as Benjo had been. When he left Leandra, she fled with him and sought refuge through the South African Council of Churches at

Wilgespruit.

Pretty found the initial time at Wilgespruit traumatic because of the police raid. Beyond that she felt that the group's stay there was beneficial and she acknowledges that their lives were saved by the refuge they were afforded. She did not find the counselling very helpful as 'all that happened was that we talked'. She found the structured leadership programmes and talks by the unions far more helpful and interesting.

She reports that she was in favour of the food boycott, as there was confusion about meal times, and the porridge was not cooked properly. Both these matters were resolved following the boycott. On being asked whether she thought that discussions should have preceded the boycott action, Pretty became very vague. She said she thought the leaders may have tried and been unsuccessful; she only became aware of the problem once the decision had been made. Everyone then participated in this decision and the group acted in concert.

When asked how she felt about the marijuana smokers at Wilgespruit, Pretty indicated that she was not on anyone's side 'because I did not know who was right or wrong. For those who smoke dagga it is their choice and when I am with them it is not on my mind.'

As regards her attitudes to violence, there is a clear split between what she thinks intellectually or rather what she sees as the correct ideas to espouse at the time, and her own gut reactions. As far as peace in the future is concerned, Pretty believes that 'we must sit down with whites and share our side of the story and they must also show us theirs. After that, an agreement must be reached.' However, when asked her own feelings towards whites, she replies, 'I would rather not have anything to do with them. It would be better if they left South Africa and moved somewhere else. They will not listen, that is why I agree with fighting. I also believe that if people put bombs in certain places they have a reason to do so. In the case where somebody has done something to them, I think this is all right.'

The contradictions in Pretty's views do not pertain only to her views towards whites. Similar discrepancies run through her discussions on the vigilantes. When asked how the vigilante problem should be solved, Pretty felt that there must be meetings and talks and peace must be established. However, in commenting on how she felt when she saw vigilantes, she said, 'I feel like fighting them. Even if one of them is in trouble or lost I will not help him because they hurt me in the past and I will not forgive them.'

Pretty is clearly an extreme example of a person whose participation in the struggle was not motivated by an internal sense of commitment. Certainly she could and did identify with the grievances that were the rallying points; on an emotional level she resonated with the moods of the group, whether jubilant, sad or angry. But neither this resonance nor her identification with the grievances reflected a deeper understanding of the issues or a commitment to the altruistic and pro-social ideals that leaders like Ricky and Sisi or even some of their other followers showed.

Her motivation to join the struggle was based on fairly transient emotions. It was not informed by a critical understanding. It is interesting that her family had no history of resistance. In general, Pretty's family life was rather bleak.

Pretty's descriptions of her early world are colourless. Her lethargy as she describes it reflects the lack of vitality, the absences and gaps she experienced. One senses that she experienced her world as something beyond her control. A sense of her own active engagement with it is lacking, as is a sense of her importance to others, and of her interconnectedness in a web of interpersonal relationships. She recalls her early relationship with her mother in terms of the household tasks she was required to perform rather than its emotional content; she does not remember being praised or valued for her successful performance of these tasks, or her contribution to the well-being and maintenance of the household.

Predominant in her reconstruction of the past are the admonitions and punishments she suffered for failure. Pretty's relationship with her harassed, overworked and pressurised mother was not a warm one. Their contact revolved around practicalities, and it seems that there was little emotional reciprocity.

Her brother, as the first-born and as the boy in the family, was the mother's favourite; he seemed to receive whatever emotional warmth there was. Pretty reports that she did not resent not having her father available to her, nor did she feel angry or hurt about her brother's privileged position. She simply accepted this as the way things were. Her passive acceptance was reinforced by the more general socialisation to which she was exposed: males, and especially first-born males, are frequently favoured children.

The acceptance of her brother's position was made easier by her intense attachment to him as her primary caretaker. While on one level she looked after him, as she had to cook and do practical chores for him, on another she looked to him for comfort and sustenance. The complexity in this relationship revealed itself at other levels.

On the one hand she idealised him and described him as good-looking, clever and popular. On the other hand she described him as harsh and unsympathetic; she felt deprived by him. He would frequently leave her alone and lock her in the house when he got bored and wanted to go out. She was forbidden by him to tell her mother about this. Despite this, she loved him, and it is a source of great grief to Pretty that her brother has not maintained consistent contact with her since their mother's death.

Both her current way of being in the world and her involvement in the struggle in 1984–86 reflect patterns that developed in her early childhood. She lacked a caretaker who would collude with the early illusion of omnipotence which children have, which fosters a belief in their abilities to master the world. She seems too soon to have lost the protective sheath provided by an empathic caretaker who mediates the encroachment of the world on the vulnerable child. As a result she lacks a sense of her own worth and does not believe in her own ability to impinge upon the world. The pattern of conformity which early in life she used as a survival strategy, still persists; her involvement in the struggle reflects this. It was not primarily inspired by her passion for an idea but by the comfort she derived from being part of a group and from conforming to it.

Pretty did not engage with the struggle to give expression to her own creativity, as did Sisi, nor did she use it to reinforce an identity that she felt fitted her own sense of self, as did Ricky. It was the vitality of the group in its singing and dancing that initially attracted her, a vitality in sharp contrast to her own inner sense of lethargy and deadness.

Her participation was also sustained both by her personal involvement with Benjo and by the way she was defined by others. Her involvement with him led her to participate in the struggle at a level beyond that at which she might normally have done. This in turn led to her being perceived by others in a particular way, and she was caught up in a momentum beyond her control.

Pretty's engagement with the struggle was therefore passive rather than active, and in this her style of participation reflected her way of engaging with life in general. As Pretty's involvement with Benjo has lapsed, so too has her active political participation. The family in which she now lives are not activists. Her current boyfriend is not an activist, but in many other aspects he resembles Benjo. Most of Pretty's relationships with boys have so far followed a similar pattern. The boys she chooses are extremely dominating and in at least two of her relationships she reports being quite severely beaten. Pretty seems thus to be re-enacting in her current life her early childhood experiences with her brother. She enters into relationships which echo his protectiveness, but also his dominance and abusiveness.

In retrospect, Pretty's participation in the struggle during 1984–86 seems in many ways to have been an incidental one; a ripple on the stream of her life despite the momentous events it encompassed. It did not serve a central integrating function in her quest for identity; on the other hand, it also did not cut across this quest in any profound way.

Certainly, having to flee the township, being detained, participating in and witnessing violence are all part of her personal history. They have left a legacy both in her psyche and in her current lived reality. She continues to encounter vigilantes in her everyday life and they still relate to her as an activist, which creates tension. This is clearly problematic and one would not wish to deny the importance of it. However, these issues do not reflect the major concerns of her life. These pertain far more to her desire to find a suitable man to marry, her desire for children and her occupational aspirations, her need to obtain what common material comforts she can. She is not alone in these concerns. There are vast numbers of youth who in 1984–86 were carried along the tide of emotion and the whirlwind liberation struggle that swept the country, but have now returned their energies to living out their lives in a more mundane context.

This group has been well described by Thandeka Gqubule, who in 1984 disguised herself as a schoolgirl and went back to school in order to study the youth. She spoke of the everyday concerns of these scholars, their desire for fashionable clothes, their concern with their appearance and love-lives. Says Gqubule (1989): 'Their conversation is not about school conditions or boycotts but about sex, designer labels and pop songs.' This is testimony to the fact that life goes on amid war, civil strife and the general adversity intrinsic to township life. To be able to continue to experience life in all its dimensions despite war is crucial to psychological well-being, and the ability of youth to return to everyday concerns is a positive sign.

Reflections on the followers

Like the leaders, the followers were highly stress-resistant. All had come from harsh backgrounds and all had sustained adversity. At the time of follow-up, all were successful in coping with this. Some coped in ways similar to the leaders, in ways similar to those described in the literature as characteristic of constitutional invulnerables (Anthony, 1987), who manage by engaging with the world and mobilising whatever resources and supports there may be in it. They use their own cognitive abilities to render their worlds 'comprehensible, manageable and meaningful' (Anthony, 1987). They seem endowed with certain natural abilities and, despite personal adversity, they are able to capitalise on the positive qualities in their lives. Isaac is a follower who fits this description. Constitutional invulnerables are, however, fairly rare in any group and the Leandra youth were no exception. About 10–12 per cent of the group could be said to fall into the category. Most of the highly stress-resistant individuals in the Leandra group, however, did not fall into this category but into various of the other categories of invulnerability described by Anthony. This was true for most of the followers who had proved themselves to be resilient. In their styles of coping, they revealed areas of vulnerability which rendered them less robust than the constitutional invulnerables. Many of the followers showed patterns of coping similar to those used by the invulnerable pseudo-heroes described by Anthony.

Pseudo-heroes deal with adversity by confrontation. Their need to confront adversity, however, has a compulsive quality about it. In this they resemble counterphobics, individuals who are deeply anxious and fearful and who deal with this by confronting danger and risk in an attempt to overcome their basic fear. Their risk-taking is, however, particularly marked where there is an audience present.

Initially this risk-taking may be functional both for themselves and for their communities, particularly in circumstances such as those which prevailed in 1984–86. Pseudo-heroes can be counted on to perform difficult and dangerous tasks unselfishly. This may be of benefit to the community and will bring the individual the affirmation and approval that is sought. However, their drive for affirmation makes the pseudo-heroes very vulnerable. They are often driven over the edge into socially disruptive behaviour in order to meet their exhibitionistic needs. They also frequently break down when the affirmation they require is not forthcoming (Anthony, 1987).

Nicholas fits in many respects the description of a counterphobic pseudo-hero. He is known for his courage and has a reputation for being fearless to the point of recklessness. Certainly his background is one which would predispose him to fear. His father, when drunk, was a very powerful and aggressive figure. Nicholas could not really take refuge in his mother whom he experienced as distanced and punitive in her own right. He felt forced to deal with the situation through the mobilisation of his own resources which, in his childhood, largely consisted of support from siblings and the peer group.

There were many pseudo-heroes in the follower group, particularly among the boys, although a lot of them were less subject to conflict than Nicholas and had found niches in which their risk-taking behaviour and acting out continued to bring them affirmation and acceptance from the broader community. There were, however, others who had not succeeded in finding such a niche and had moved over the edge into socially disruptive behaviour. They had either broken down and become casualties or were substance abusers or, more commonly, gangsters or comtsotsis. In this latter group the pseudo-heroes could find affirmation for their risk-taking behaviour in the restricted circle of the gang sub-culture. One such person was Silas, whose biography will be outlined in the discussion of the anti-social group, a grouping which also has its fair share of pseudo-heroes and sociopathic invulnerables (Anthony, 1987).

Though there were relatively few truly sociopathic invulnerables in the follower group, a number of individuals evidenced some of the characteristics of the sociopathic invulnerables described by Anthony. Sociopathic invulnerables maintain their own level of functioning through isolation and withdrawal. They deal with hardship and trauma by insulating themselves and cutting themselves off from their own emotional responses. They show little psychological reaction to events that might profoundly affect others. Their capacity to engage intimately with their environments is blunted. They may go through the motions, but they never really establish themselves within an intimate network of interrelationships. They do not really identify with or dedicate themselves to an overriding principle or ideal. Because of their failure to invest themselves emotionally in the world, their emotional response to adversity is diminished. They invest less so they lose less when things go wrong, and they are thus able to sustain more without succumbing to psychological breakdown. However, if criteria of psychological functioning are applied which not only depend on the absence of overt symptomatology but on the presence of positive attributes like the ability to love, to play and to be altruistic, the sociopathic invulnerables do not qualify as true invulnerables because of this basic fault in their capacity to invest themselves emotionally in their world. They may hide this inability through external conformity in which they play the social roles expected of them, but without real feeling.

To some extent Pretty fits this description. She is to a degree cut off from her emotions. There is a certain flatness in her description of her losses. When she talks of the death of her parents, there is no real sharpness or intensity of emotion evident. Similarly, the momentous events in Leandra and at Wilgespruit seem to have left far less of an imprint on her than would have been anticipated. In her description of her reactions at Mayisa's funeral there is also a sense that Pretty operates in the world by making the appropriate response without really feeling deeply about most things.

She has also failed to establish herself in a network of truly intimate interpersonal relationships. Although she is part of the group at school, she has no really close friends. There is nobody in whom she feels she can confide. She acknowledges the kindness and concern of her friend's family but feels emotionally distanced from them.

However, there are certain important differences between Pretty's mode of being in the world and that of a fully sociopathic invulnerable. Sociopathic invulnerables operate by clearly defining themselves and their limitations and refusing to budge, whatever pressures are placed upon them. There is a certain rigidity about them. Pretty copes by using a strategy which is diametrically opposed to that of the sociopathic individual. She adopts a passive mode of being in the world and allows her identity to be moulded by others to an excessive degree. While the sociopathic invulnerable confronts the storms of adversity by becoming rocklike, Pretty confronts adversity by becoming a leaf that drifts upon the tides, thereby remaining intact.

It is a lack of true emotional involvement that Pretty and the other conformists like her share in common with Anthony's invulnerable sociopaths. This lack of involvement prompts the conformists and sociopathic invulnerables to take on the colours of their current environment. As a result they become as contained and healthy or as uncontained and unhealthy as their outer world.

Certainly, in the household of her friend's family Pretty functions at a more successful level than she did in her own home. Nevertheless, she remains without a clear sense of herself and her limitations; she continues to allow others in her environment to define her self for her, a process in which she seeks refuge. Yet it cannot be denied that this mode of adaptation has allowed her to cope with severe stress without breaking down.

This conformist mode of coping was characteristic of a fair number of individuals in the follower group, especially among the girls. In regard to the boys in the follower group, the style of coping described by Anthony as characteristic of the pseudo-heroes was preferred to the conformist mode. Both styles of coping, however, allowed individuals to deal with very high levels of stress without breaking down. Thus, whatever value judgments one might pass on them from the outside, they are both very adaptive modes of coping with the particular world in which these youth live.

3 Psychological Vulnerability of Youth at War

By definition, psychological casualties are individuals who have been so overwhelmed by their circumstances that they can no longer function in everyday life within the parameters and constraints laid down by their own communities. This inability to function may manifest itself in many forms. In the Leandra group, some protested against their lot by acting out and becoming anti-social. Others attempted to anaesthetise and insulate themselves from their psychic pain through substance abuse. Yet others were unable to block out their pain and were so overwhelmed that their everyday life was disrupted by psychosomatic symptomatology, anxiety and depression. A myriad of factors influenced whether or not individuals became casualties and what form this took. Some of these factors will become clearer in the following case vignettes.

THE CASUALTIES

Matthew

Matthew was one of the 20 per cent of those interviewed who showed clinical signs of depression and anxiety. He also manifested a number of psychosomatic symptoms, including headaches and sleeplessness which, he complained, disrupted his daily life. He often needed to lie down and found it very difficult to motivate himself. Given the severity of his symptoms Matthew was classified as a psychological casualty. He encapsulates many of the characteristics of those who fell into this category.

At Wilgespruit, Matthew was clearly a leader, not a charismatic leader of Ricky's standing, but one who nevertheless commanded respect. The staff at Wilgespruit all reported positively on Matthew and found him to be reasonable and reliable. Many of the group seemed to use him as a resource person; he occupied a position of second-tier leadership. He was self-assured and presented in a pleasant but self-contained fashion.

At the time of the follow-up interview he was still friendly and co-operative. There was, however, little of his previous confidence. He was obviously anxious and agitated and needed to take frequent toilet and smoke breaks. He complained of constant headaches, chronic fatigue and sleeplessness. He was still very verbal and artic-ulate, but it was clearly difficult for him to focus his thoughts and ideas. He seemed fragile and close to tears. Despair and disillusion-ment rather than anger or resentment were the predominant emotions.

It was clear that he felt he had invested a great deal of himself in rebellion and resistance with little return. He believed that liberation was certainly not on the horizon and felt persecuted by his label of activist. He had to leave school as a result of being perceived by the authorities to be a ringleader, and his police record for public vio-lence obstructed his search for employment.

Matthew is one of seven children. He reports that he was reason-ably happy for the first sixteen years of his life. He was the oldest child and got on well with all his siblings. His parents had a stable relationship and his mother looked after the children at home. Life became difficult for Matthew when his father died in 1984. The family was destitute. He recalls that he used to go out to school and then return home without even 'a crust of bread to eat'.

It was at about this time that he was approached by a group of 'comrades' who asked him to join their organisation, which was affiliated to the UDF. He was particularly bitter during this time owing to the fact that scholars, including himself, were being used to clean up the township. Matthew felt strongly that this work should have been given to the unemployed like his mother, and that scholars had been used in order to avoid having to pay anyone to do it. He had long been angry over the discrepancies between conditions in the township and neighbouring white suburbs; the lack of electricity, sewerage, street lights and other facilities all irked him, but this was the final straw. He joined a youth organisation and soon assumed a leadership position.

This was not Matthew's first exposure to political education. As early as 1981, when he was thirteen years old, he was friendly with some older adolescents who belonged to AZAPO. However, what he perceived to be their anti-white sentiment put him off and he could never really commit himself to the organisation. The ideas and principles of the UDF had far more appeal for him and he joined it in 1984.

In December 1985 Matthew was arrested and tortured. He was taken during school hours; a policeman called him over and, not believing that he would simply be detained there and then, he went to speak to him. He was taken to prison and interrogated about underground movements in the township. He reports that he was beaten and put in a cell with a police dog that bit him. He had no information to give and the police eventually let him go. The experience did not deter him but only made him more determined and committed to the struggle. It also increased his stature within the organisation. He became more involved in its activities and was detained again six months later.

When Mayisa was killed in January 1986, Matthew was not present. He was in Bethal in hiding, fleeing a public violence charge. He returned to the township but vigilante activity forced him again to flee. Since the Wilgespruit experience, Matthew has remained involved in youth organisations. In this time he has undergone significant and bitter experiences: two of his friends have been killed. One was shot in his home and another was killed in an incident of public violence.

He complains that he finds it difficult to concentrate. This difficulty, coupled with his constant headaches, interferes with his day-to-day activities. He needs to spend time in the day resting because he gets so tired. He indicates that his problems on this level started shortly after Wilgespruit. It took a great deal of probing to establish that the precipitating factor was a conflict with his mother, who has never really understood or supported his political activities. She worries about him and fears for his safety.

During the stay at Wilgespruit, when Matthew went out on a secret visit to see her, she confronted him with the implications of his activities, pointing to the harassment and hardship the family was suffering as a result, and reminded him of his filial responsibility to support it since his father had died. He was struck by how frail and ill she looked, and in that critical moment he promised to curtail his activities. On his return to Wilgespruit he could not discuss this or confide in anyone. He felt deeply ashamed that he had somehow betrayed the cause. Yet he felt that he had had no choice, that he was trapped. Shortly after this he began to suffer bad headaches and sleeplessness. He felt paralysed and lame, and indeed this sense of physical paralysis paralleled the psychological immobility forced on him by being presented with two equally compelling but conflicting claims on his loyalty.

In the face of this conflict Matthew has to make huge efforts simply to mobilise himself to get through the day. In real terms he has tried to strike a compromise with both commitments. He has remained within the struggle but not without ambivalence and an expressed desire at times simply to escape it all. He has also joined the long lines of the unemployed, seeking work. His search for employment is, however, proving to be a fruitless and demoralising task. He feels desperate about this as he sees his family continuing to suffer. He feels impotent in his inability to assist them, in view of his responsibility as a male and as the first-born in the family, especially having given his word to his mother to fulfil these duties. As the situation perpetuates itself, Matthew is becoming increasingly depressed, desperate and unable to function.

Despite all these hardships, Matthew, far from emerging as a hardened, brutal person, presents as a compassionate, caring human being. These qualities were evident not only in discussing members of his family and friends, but also those of whom he might have disapproved, including policemen.

On being questioned, Matthew expressed complete opposition to the principle of attacking soft targets. He sees human life as something to be valued and protected. He agrees that violence may at times be necessary, but believes it should be directed against objects, not people. He opposes violence against people for two reasons. Firstly, it is more difficult than meets the eye to separate friend from foe. He quotes the case of a policeman who was recently convicted of being a member of the ANC. Furthermore, he believes that even if people do become genuine informers and supporters of the state, it is very difficult to assess their personal guilt. Clearly identifying with their dilemma, he talks of how poverty can force people to act against their principles in order to survive and to protect their families. He himself has never been tempted to follow this path because of deep personal loyalties to individuals in the organisation and because of the support he draws from them. However, he can understand how others get inveigled into such situations.

His own desperate plight has also given him more insight into the motivation of those who leave the country to join the armed wing of the ANC. At first he felt that these individuals were running away from the real grassroots issues. He did not see them in idealised terms or believe them to be heroes, as did many of his counterparts. He believed rather that they were taking an easy option and was critical of their desertion of family and friends. Now he believes they were driven to this option, not only by their despair at enduring oppression, but also because of their immediate material needs.

Matthew's external circumstances are objectively very painful. He has not, however, chosen to deal with them through splitting and projection; he has not split his internal world and divided people intra-psychically into friend and foe, idealising the one and vilifying the other. He has chosen to live with complexity. Furthermore, he has not identified an external enemy, whether it be policeman or informer, against whom to rage, to express his accumulated pain and anger. In choosing not to eject his feelings in this way Matthew is left with the burden of experiencing his own pain and discomfort. He has plumbed his depths and identified his own potential for betrayal and faithlessness. In this lies his strength. However, it also blocks any escape he might have from the misery of his material world by not allowing him simply to act out his feelings.

In reflecting upon Matthew's position we see many dilemmas arise. He is indeed a casualty: he carries a burden of pain which makes his life uncomfortable and stressful. Yet if we use different criteria for evaluation, Matthew is not a casualty but one of the true survivors in this study. He has remained, despite all the odds, humane and compassionate. He bears the wounds of this in his physical being, in his headaches, his fatigue, his sleeplessness. He has chosen to feel and to articulate his pain rather than to deny it or to act it out. He is paying the price for this, but perhaps it is in the likes of Matthew that true hope for post-apartheid society resides.

Benjy

Benjy presented as a psychological casualty both at Wilgespruit and at follow-up. Prior to Wilgespruit he had been exposed to multiple hardships, including being orphaned, and transferred from foster home to foster home, and was familiar with the hardships of poverty and ghetto life. He had used the struggle in an attempt to escape the pain of his life, but found that his involvement compounded rather than solved his problems.

At Wilgespruit Benjy was fourteen years old. Throughout the interview he sat with his eyes downcast. The only signs of animation occurred when his current foster family was discussed. He then

repeatedly communicated that he wished to return to them immediately. When it was indicated to him that it was not safe to return,
he assumed an almost foetal position in the chair, arms folded, legs
drawn up, head down.

The counsellor who interviewed him at the time described him as
'a person without solace'. He was also very slow and seemed to
have difficulty understanding what was being asked of him. He had
little idea of the aims or meaning of the struggle. It appeared that he
had joined the group because it gave him something to do and, at
least initially, because he felt some sort of belonging. This soon dissipated, however, as his slowness and clumsiness irritated his comrades and they lost patience with him. Nevertheless, he was desperate for group acceptance and there was little doubt that he
would have gone along with whatever the group did, however
mindlessly, in order to obtain their approval.

At the time of follow-up it was not possible to interview Benjy.
His previous placement had broken down and he had relocated to a
township some distance from Leandra. However, key informants
indicated that subsequent to his return from Wilgespruit he had
abandoned the cause. He was considered to be too slow and unin-
telligent to participate meaningfully and his presence became
increasingly irksome. In his placement, his dependence and rivalry
with other siblings had contributed to its breakdown, as had the
general level of hardship faced by his foster family.

It was very difficult to establish much about Benjy's biological family. His father, it appears, abandoned his mother before he was
born, and she in turn abandoned him soon after this. He was left
with relatives who were unwilling and unable to bear the financial
burden, and his transfer from household to household began very
early in life.

At the time of the interview he himself could not keep track of his
placements. The degree of his deprivation was reflected in the reasons he gave for enjoying his placement at that time. He was in a
family of nine siblings yet, unlike the previous placements, he was
not 'treated as a servant' and made to wait on and run errands for
the others. He was served food along with the others and was not
'always last'. He was also not always given the left-overs. He felt the
mother of the family took some notice of him and cared about him.
It was quite clear that he had formed a bond with her. This makes
the ultimate failure of this placement even more tragic. It is uncer-

tain what has become of Benjy, but the possibilities of a successful resolution of his situation are limited.

Benjy is but one of thousands of South Africa's children who succumb to the misery, poverty and hardship of their lot. It is uncertain what the cause of his evident slowness was, but it is probable that very early adversity, which may well have included malnutrition, contributed to it. He was certainly not the apple of anyone's eye during his early childhood. He was not able to engage with any of his caretakers or cajole them into looking after him. His world offered little opportunity for secure attachments. There was no special person in his life and he possessed no special talent which might have endowed him with a measure of resilience. His constitution, his early family life and his life circumstances all conspired to undermine rather than to facilitate resistance to stress.

Joining the struggle offered no solution to his problems. Indeed it alienated him still further as he became more of an outsider. Furthermore, it placed him in an untenable situation in which he was cut off from what he perceived to be his only source of solace and comfort. To say that Benjy was a victim of the struggle would be a misnomer. He was one of life's casualties long before he was swept up in the events of 1986.

The adverse environment created by an oppressive system hostile to family life, designed to keep large sections of the population in poverty and isolated in ghettos, proved overwhelming. His only hope lies in the success of the very struggle which has so compounded his problems in the short term. Even so, it is doubtful that Benjy will be in a position to benefit from the fruits of this struggle should it eventually succeed. His damage seems so profound as to be beyond repair, other than through intensive re-parenting and emotional support. The establishment on a broad scale of such rehabilitative services in South Africa lies even further in the future than the liberation in the cause of which Benjy joined the struggle.

While Benjy's case probably represents an extreme example of deprivation and hardship, it is not atypical. The struggle attracted many of the township's emotional cripples. By its nature it could not really offer these deeply troubled persons any real solace and comfort. It could only compound their trials and tribulations, and for many of them it did.

Hundreds of youth who really needed the comfort of a home and the benefit of continued parental support were forced to flee both their families and their communities. Similarly, hundreds of youth were exposed to confrontations with violence, brutality, injury and death. There is no doubt that these traumas in and of themselves resulted in many suffering post-traumatic stress, depression, anxiety and psychosomatic illness. However, it is important to recognise that these events were superimposed upon conditions that were in general extraordinarily adverse.

Youth in South Africa's townships are generally exposed to high levels of violence. A study by the author in conjunction with Rai Turton and Fathima Moosa (1991) revealed that in the ordinary course of events, 80–90 per cent of a group of school-going youth in Alexandra township reported witnessing, in a one-year period, at least one incident of rape, murder or assault which was not politically motivated. The crime rate in the townships is excessively high as is the rate of all the other social problems usually associated with ghettos, including alcoholism and family violence, conflict and breakdown. These problems, combined with the unremitting poverty which underpins them, are the backdrop against which the political violence erupted.

The findings of this study with regard to the clinical casualties are similar to those of overseas researchers. They indicate unequivocally that while the factor that best promotes survival is the opportunity for secure bonding and attachment, the factor which undermines it most is quite simply poverty. Poverty not only creates its own hardships which have to be dealt with and overcome, but it also acts to restrict the range of any potential solutions the individual might generate. It therefore throws up major problems while at the same time limiting their possible resolution.

Although there are victims like Benjy and many like Matthew who have survived and retained their humanity and control of their overt behaviour, there are also many who are struggling and who have survived less well. An example of such a person is Silas who, despite himself, cannot contain his anger and aggression. His case vignette follows.

Tsotsis, Comtsotsis and Substance Abusers

Approximately a third of the original Leandra group were classified at the time of follow-up as tsotsis, comtsotsis or substance abusers by key informants. There was considerable overlap between the tsotsi–comtsotsi group and the substance-abuse group. Individuals who were tsotsis or comtsotsis and who were also substance abusers were placed in the former category. The term 'tsotsi' is used in black communities to describe persons who consistently engage in anti-social behaviour including theft, gangsterism, intimidation and harassment of the community; comtsotsis are those who attempt to justify their behaviour as legitimate political activity. Even more than the tsotsis, this group is perceived negatively by the community.

Silas

During his sojourn at Wilgespruit, Silas was described by the staff as a ringleader. He was a central figure in the marijuana-smoking incident and was thought to be a generally disruptive influence. He was described at the time as having the 'physique of a boxer and being as brave as a lion', but also as irresponsible and lacking in self-control. He had a great deal of influence in the group because he was a comedian; he used humour to cajole the others into breaking boundaries and behaving in an uncontained way. If humour failed, he resorted to intimidation and harassment to assert his authority. He was involved in numerous physical fights at Wilgespruit and was perceived to be emotionally volatile and short-tempered. On interview, his volatility, humour and charm were all evident, as was a softness and sensitivity which was not immediately apparent in the Wilgespruit period. His anti-social behaviour had, however, persisted, as had his marijuana smoking; he was awaiting trial for assault at the time of the follow-up interview.

At this interview Silas presented as a tall, well-built young man, twenty-two years of age. He had a ready smile and joked with the interpreter, who was able to tease him and enter into easy banter. A number of scars on his face and arms were apparent. On being asked their origin, he made it clear that they resulted from injuries he had sustained in a variety of skirmishes.

Silas related easily to the interview situation. He seemed surprisingly eager to please, and very desirous of approval and affection. There was no air of machismo or defensiveness about him. He answered the questions with an astounding openness and candour. He was not out of touch with his emotions, as may have been anticipated. He seemed rather to be undefended and to be able to contain depths of feelings which were keenly experienced.

He is one of seven children, the youngest of five his mother had by her first husband. She subsequently had two children by her

second husband, all of whom lived in the same house. Silas's biological father, of whom he has no substantial memories, left home
when he was four years old. As a child he tended to idealise his
absent father; he spoke of his childhood desire to find him. He was
disillusioned when he succeeded in tracking him down, only to find
he was a dissolute alcoholic with no interest in his son.

Silas describes his stepfather as a cool and distant man. He never
really invested in him emotionally and felt little grief when he died
in 1988. His mother, with whom he continues to have an intense
and conflict-bound relationship, is a more significant figure in his
life. She is a well-respected *inyanga*. She is depicted as an enor-
mously powerful and persecutory force in Silas's life. She was very
strict and frequently used to beat him with a belt. He rates these
beatings as very minor punishments, however, compared to the psychological sanctions he endured. When she was angry with him for
some infringement of the household rules, such as helping himself
to food or drink without permission, she would threaten to bewitch
him and call down the wrath of the ancestors, or beseech them to
withdraw their protection and allow evil to befall him. Silas reports
that he was terrified of his mother in these moments, and still is.

In addition to being intimidated by his mother it seems that he
also had a poor relationship with his older siblings, all of whom
were boys. As the youngest he seemed to be at their beck and call;
he recalls being sent out on errands for them, often having to walk
long distances in cold and wet weather.

He started school when he was eight years old but was forced to
leave four years later. Financial hardship made it impossible for the
family to continue to support him. It was at this point that he sought
his biological father in the hope that he would contribute to his
education. He was disappointed. For the next two years he simply
remained at home, helping his mother and being a lackey for his
brothers, until he joined the struggle in 1985. He was inducted into
it by one of the youth leaders who approached him, explained what
the struggle was about, and invited him to come to a meeting that
night to discuss issues in the township. Silas did so and began
attending regularly. In time he became a highly valued member of
the group because of his physical strength and bravery. When public violence broke out in Leandra in 1985, he was heavily involved.
He was observed throwing a petrol-bomb at a council building, was
arrested, convicted of public violence, and fined.

This episode of violence and the subsequent brush with the law were not the first in his life. He had been arrested for assault when he was sixteen years old and held in custody for six weeks because no application was made for his release. When the case was in fact heard it was dismissed. As he spoke of this episode Silas became very tearful and in fact had to leave the room to regain control. It had begun with a disagreement over a girlfriend with someone in the township whom Silas knew well. The argument had intensified and Silas attacked his adversary with an axe, badly injuring him as a result of a blow to the head.

Nor was this incident his first skirmish. He reports that for as long as he can remember he has had difficulty restraining his temper and his inclination to physical violence. However, it was the first which left his victim permanently harmed. He began to drink after this episode, in an attempt to forget it. He reports that he feels great remorse about the incident, for even in the moment he knew that he was much stronger than his adversary, that he had an unfair advantage. He is haunted by the fear and pain he recollects seeing in his victim's eyes. Apart from his guilt and regret, he also fears retaliation to this day, either directly from the victim's relatives or indirectly through bewitchment. Silas was in fact attacked by three of his victim's brothers, who ambushed him as he was returning home from an outing. He ran but they gave chase and cornered him. He had to fight his way out of the situation, stabbing two of them in the process and being stabbed himself. He was not subject to any further attacks but still fears that reprisals might be exacted.

On his release from prison after this incident, his mother took him to an *inyanga* near White River. She felt he needed to undergo ritual purification and also to be protected from harm which might befall him through bewitchment. This helped him initially and allayed some of his anxieties. He believes that had his mother not taken these precautions his position would have been worse, but he is still troubled by the event.

Silas does not feel guilty about all the skirmishes and attacks in which he has been involved. His sense of guilt or lack of it seems to be determined by whether he believes the victim is an enemy of the people, in which case he can see his aggression as having a purpose beyond itself. It also depends on whether he believes himself to have held an unfair advantage or not. Thus Silas's response to his own violence is dictated by his beliefs about its legitimacy.

He is currently charged with the assault of a municipal policeman, or 'green bean'. He feels no guilt about the fact that he shot this man. This is quite clear when he recounts the episode. His voice is firm and his anger palpable. The incident occurred when the policeman apprehended him on his way home from a shebeen. He pointed his revolver at Silas, who gave way to anger and attacked him, wresting the weapon away. The policeman was shot and wounded in the process. He believes his attack was justified both in self-defence and as a social act of defiance against one who was intrinsically an enemy of the people. He is afraid of going to jail and has once again sought the help of an *inyanga* recommended by his mother. He does not, however, have any intrusive thoughts or nightmares about this event. Unlike the former episode, Silas believes that his aggression was justified and that it served some purpose.

He remains committed to the struggle. He has had several jobs since leaving school and in all of them he has been an active member of a union. He has, however, not been able either to enter the leadership or to retain his job because of his alcohol abuse.

Despite his alcohol abuse and violence, Silas has managed to sustain an intimate relationship with a young woman who lives with him, his mother and his youngest brother in their communal home. He has two children of whom he speaks with fondness, but he is concerned about his inability to support them financially. His overwhelming anxiety at the moment is for the welfare of his family should he be jailed. It seems inevitable that he will be, and it is uncertain how this will influence his life in the long term.

There is no doubt that Silas's behaviour is frequently very anti-social. He also has a major substance-abuse problem over which he has little control. Despite this, he does not present as a brutal person. On the contrary there is a disarming openness and vulnerability about him.

He is a very dependent person. He has not been nurtured or cared for and carries the scars about with him. There is an easily apparent affect hunger, a need for approval and affection, a fear of criticism. In his fear of and sensitivity to criticism Silas is the prototypical narcissistic personality. His self-esteem and, indeed, his sense of self are so tenuous that they are easily shattered. He feels humiliated and rejected very easily. He is even capable of experiencing the failure by others to perceive the world as he does, as rejection.

When he is crossed or offended he cannot easily retain his sense of self. In his description of such experiences it is as if he falls into a sudden maelstrom of emotion which destroys control. It is no longer

Silas who is angry and acting on this anger, but the anger itself which becomes him. There is no sense of the self as an agent; it is only when the paroxysm of emotion has played itself out or something cuts across it that his sense of self returns. In the assault upon his first victim, the fear and pain shown at the moment of impact shocked him back into his sense of self. In other instances, the emotion simply played itself out.

On the whole, Silas finds these experiences deeply disturbing. The exception to this is when his anger, either fortuitously or by design, is activated in a situation in which others would approve of his actions. Thus the attack on the 'green bean' was not experienced as disturbing. Silas is happy to allow his natural courage, which is fuelled by reserves of anger, to be used by his comrades. Their approval pleases him. Furthermore, attacks carried out against perceived enemies, even if they occur in a blind fury, do not transgress any of Silas's superego dictates, in terms of which he undoubtedly operates.

He is not a psychopath. His behaviour is frequently brutal but he is not without remorse or guilt, nor is his remorse simply a sentimental reflex. It is discriminating rather than amorphous. There are situations in which he experiences it and situations in which he does not: his guilt is mobilised within certain parameters.

He is clearly a victim of a fate that was not benign enough to sustain his integrity. He seems by nature to be a sensitive, impassioned person. He has known fear and psychological persecution and manipulation from an early age. He has known disappointment as his dreams of completing his education were smashed. He has also known gross forms of physical abuse. Despite this, he has retained his sense of humour, his charm and openness.

It is not that life has hardened Silas and made him callous. It seems rather as if its roughness has acted abrasively, eroding the protective layers that in normal circumstances stand between the self and the world. Stimuli from the external world, particularly rejection, humiliation or attempts at domination, penetrate very quickly, and he has no ability to modulate their impact. In turn they evoke uncontained, unprocessed emotion which is acted out rather than felt, symbolised or articulated.

The future for Silas looks bleak. His family, which was initially unable to provide an environment protective enough to consolidate a sense of self, is certainly not protective now. His stepfather's death and the jailing of one of his siblings have left the family in crisis. His own almost inevitable incarceration will intensify the crisis.

Imprisonment will certainly provoke further crises for Silas. The relative unavailability of alcohol might help him on one level. However, it is almost certain that Silas will very quickly be involved in conflict in the ungentle, provocative environment jails generate.

It is not certain how his wife, who is young and active, will sustain a prolonged absence. Should she leave him during this period, it would certainly constitute a very major assault on his fragile self-esteem. Whatever the bleakness of his past circumstances, his future stretches out before him unremittingly.

Altogether it is remarkable that he has retained any capacity at all for caring and commitment. Yet he has these capacities, together with an equally remarkable vulnerability which, though in one sense it is his greatest strength, is also his greatest weakness. It increases his need to relate, while amplifying his inability to defend himself from the slights of the world. It seems inevitable that he responds through violence and the self-anaesthetisation of alcohol abuse.

Len

At an overt level, Len presented with many of the same characteristics as Silas. He had a history of violent outbursts and was known to be a substance abuser, of both alcohol and marijuana, but more particularly the latter. At the time of the follow-up interview he presented, like Silas, as somewhat battle-scarred and battered. He had a number of clearly evident welts along his arms and face, most of which had been sustained in running battles with the police and vigilantes rather than in more personal vendettas.

At Wilgespruit Len did not command the same kind of presence that Silas did. He did not clown around to manipulate attention, or make any real bid for leadership; he did have a certain residual status within the group because of his blood ties with a prominent community leader. Len seemed secure in this as well as in his reputation of being 'somebody one did not cross'. He was also one of the figures implicated in the marijuana-smoking episode and was generally not trusted by the staff. He was, however, regarded by his peers as a respected member of the struggle, and a brave comrade. By the time of the follow-up interview he had been labelled a comtsotsi by key informants, a term which carries a very high pejorative value.

At the interview Len presented as a morose, angry nineteen-year-old. He did not really enter into the situation and remained hostile and suspicious throughout. His resentment of authorities in general and whites in particular was evident throughout, both in the responses he gave and in his relationship to the interviewer.

Len was one of four children. He was the second-born, with an older brother as well as a younger stepbrother and stepsister. His mother died when he was six years old. He recalls her death and indicates that it was traumatic. He says that his relationship with his father was without conflict and he got on tolerably well with his stepmother. However, he mentions with resentment that she always favoured her own children.

Len's difficulties in the broader environment began early. Some of his first memories are of avoiding school. He did not get on with the other children and used to duck out and run away as often as he could. He also had a very punitive teacher when he began school and this did not help matters much. It set the tone for an unhappy school career. After his first year he dropped out and did not return for four years. He then went back for two.

He joined the struggle at fifteen, and by the time of Wilgespruit one year later, had already been forced into hiding twice. He had taken a very high profile in Leandra, prior to the stay at Wilgespruit, not so much because of his own involvement in the struggle, but because his uncle was a prominent activist. In fact it was through his uncle that many of the Leandra youth were enlisted. It was through him that Len too became involved in the struggle.

He reports that this changed his life. Before then he had felt impotently angry about his own life situation and that of his people. His involvement in the struggle gave him a sense of purpose and put him in touch with a network of people to whom he could relate. It is clear that within this group he had a degree of status and thrived on it. He became less isolated and withdrawn and began to delve into himself and find abilities and talents that were valued. He discovered a courage and physical strength which he had not known he possessed.

Len was one of the youth present when Chief Mayisa was killed, and one of the group most sought after by the vigilantes. In fact, in the time between Mayisa's death and his funeral, he was accosted by a group of vigilantes and threatened with death. He was surrounded and given the choice of death by shooting, stabbing or burning. He was only saved by the intervention of one of the vigilantes who pleaded for him on the grounds of his age. This vigilante had played soccer with Len previously and had some sense of affiliation with him. The vigilantes released him on the strength of these pleas, but not before he had been beaten with a sjambok and stabbed. The scars from these wounds were evident at the time of follow-up and will remain with Len as permanent reminders of his ordeal.

Nor was this the only incident of its kind. He was accosted and beaten on at least two other occasions. When he talks of these episodes he does so in a flat, unemotional way. In fact he does not evidence much emotion at all, whether he is talking about his own treatment at the hands of the vigilantes or whether he is talking about the death of Mayisa. Despite his unemotional tone of voice, the content of his communication conveys deeply felt anger and bitterness. He clearly has a desire for revenge and retaliation against the vigilantes, the police, the 'system', and whites in general. He believes in attacks on both hard and soft targets and approves of violence. His body language also speaks of pent-up anger and frustration. He seldom relaxes and there is a tension in him which persists without regard to the nature of the material he is discussing.

Len claims that he is still involved in the struggle. He is sufficiently in touch to recognise that his activities are not approved of by many of his former comrades but he sees this as reflecting their naiveté and lack of understanding of the issues. He does not believe that his own behaviour is in any way out of line.

He feels that his earlier colleagues have betrayed both himself and his uncle. His uncle has also fallen from grace after he was accused of being a sell-out when his daughter married a policeman. Len believes that the current disfavour he finds himself in is linked to his uncle's situation. He is probably correct in this: his situation does seem to fluctuate with that of his uncle.

Len carries out many of his activities in a group context. However, he does not operate in a well-defined gang as such. The group is very loosely constructed and its membership is in constant flux. He does not have the charisma or social skill to weld a gang together. It would seem rather that he joins in with loosely constituted groups of comtsotsis who coerce people into giving them money and resources, ostensibly for political ends.

Members of the group reinforce each another's perception of the legitimacy of their activities. They provide one another with support and satisfy needs for affiliation and group approval. Most members of these loose groupings are unemployed and many come together to pass the time as well as to generate income. It would seem from key informants that a fair number of these individuals are socially inept. When not in the groupings, they lead isolated lives in which marijuana smoking and alcohol abuse play a large part. Some, like Len, did have greater or lesser status while they were committed to the struggle, but lost it either because of their own personal problems or because they were unable to meet the challenges presented by the movement away from relatively militant forms of association to more systematic planning and organisation. Like Len, they are nostalgic for the good old days of excitement and action when their own positions and roles were more clearly defined. They show an inability to return to mundane life, to forge a new identity for themselves within their changed circumstances.

Len's early life in many ways seemed less deprived than those of many others in the Leandra group. His parents had a stable relationship and his mother was available to him in his early years. His father earned better than the fathers of many others in the study. However, he did sustain a very severe early trauma in the death of his mother. During the interview his pain was evident. He clearly relates to this event as one which precipitated his exit, in psychological terms, from paradise. Seen in retrospect, her death marked the beginning of his trials. He connects his early school experiences with it, with not having her to protect him. It would seem too that he chose this arena to act out and to give expression to his pain. His behaviour was not understood and he became increasingly withdrawn. It was only in his teenage years that his uncle emerged as a significant presence, offering affirmation and purpose. Len leapt at the offer. Suddenly he found himself respected; he had a place in the world. He did not re-enter paradise, but at least he moved away from the depression and despair of his isolation. He found abilities in himself which had lain dormant and was able to emerge from his twilight zone into a more positive emotional space.

What he found was not always pleasant, as his encounters with the vigilantes attest. However, it was at least within a context of connectedness and within a web of meaningful interpersonal relationships that he confronted this trauma. It was this kind of connectedness which had so abruptly been cut off when his mother died and, in a new form, allowed him to flourish in his early teens. However, it was not to last. Just as his uncle's status had initially given him a place in the community, so too did his uncle's fall from grace lead to his being alienated once more. As Len's fortunes changed through events outside of his control, he was unable to use his own resources to resist the turning of the tide, to trade on the contributions he had made in his own right. He could not assert his own identity but succumbed to depression at the initial loss of status. He became angry and accusatory, and this attitude further alienated people. He thus re-established for himself his old pattern of isolation and withdrawal, but this time it was superimposed upon a desire for affiliation and affirmation which he could no longer successfully repress. He was forced, therefore, to seek fulfilment of those needs in loose groupings of other misfits like himself. Like many others, he created around himself all the trappings of the days of his participation in the struggle: he returned to the slogans, the rhetoric, the group activity, but not the idealism or the purpose of this participation.

THE LEANDRA STUDY IN INTERNATIONAL CONTEXT

In wars, the dead and the physically injured have always been counted, but it is only recently that psychological casualties have generated much interest. Concern about the impact of war on children and youth is even more recent. Only in the last twenty years has there been an upsurge of interest in the effects of war and civil strife on the development of children and youth. This reflects a new set of values in relation to psychological development and a new way of conceptualising it. In Western post-industrial societies, childhood and adolescence have come to be seen as times of privilege and entitlement, with a tremendous stress placed on trying to understand young people and on protecting them from hardship. This, however, has not always been the case.

The idea that children are vulnerable and in need of special care was only enshrined in international humanitarian law after World War Two. The Geneva Convention of 1949 acknowledged the importance of the family in providing care and protection for children and therefore took into account the affective tie of children with their families, particularly their mothers. In its emphasis on family unity and the emotional importance of the biological mother, the convention reflected relatively new values. In previous eras it was certainly not believed that children suffered any ill effects from being separated from their primary caretakers or from lack of continuity in caretaking arrangements.

It is clear, then, that definitions of childhood and child-rearing practices and the treatment accorded children are both culturally and historically bound. But this does not, however, exonerate one from the obligation of making value judgments. An argument for cultural sensitivity and for attempting to understand the values that inform a particular judgment should not be taken as an argument for extreme cultural relativity. Be that as it may, although hardship itself can be read in various ways, the notion that chronic hardship or acutely traumatic experiences are automatically or even frequently psychologically damaging must be thrown into question. Their effects have to be considered in the light of the context in which they occur.

It is increasingly recognised that not only do most people survive multiple hardships, but some even seem to be strengthened by them. Nevertheless, this should not be read to imply that these hardships have no negative consequences at all. They clearly do. Certainly in the Leandra group 50 per cent of the group showed signs of psychological disturbance at the time of follow-up. However, the criteria by which psychological disturbance is defined have largely been developed by first world scientists whose values and worldviews are inevitably and inextricably woven into them. This is problematic in that situations have frequently arisen in which what is deemed culturally undesirable is labelled pathological.

This tendency to label the undesirable as pathological was very clearly seen in the South African press following reports of widespread 'unrest' in the townships. Protest and civil disobedience among the black youth was quickly criminalised and labelled pathological both by the press and by professional bodies, including those which intended to ally themselves with the youth. This labelling often occurred obliquely through the expression of fears that a brutalised pathological generation was being spawned or that the youth were being irreparably damaged. It was particularly noteworthy at this time, however, that only black youth were labelled pathological. Their white counterparts in the South African Defence Force, many of whom were also engaged in and were witnesses to acts of extreme violence, were not seen to be a generation at risk to the same degree, although infrequent references were made to the general culture of violence in South Africa. This particular emphasis on black youth seemed to reflect a common bias toward condoning

violence within formal state structures, while criminalising or patho-
logising violence occurring outside them, regardless of the relative
justice of each cause.

Notions of criminality and pathology in any event lend themselves
to bias. They are extremely problematic concepts within psychology, which has no way of defining them outside of what is normative or desirable in a particular culture. This dilemma, which
confronts psychology in general, was clearly one which the present
project shared. In assessing the impact of civil strife on the Leandra
group, value decisions had to be made about the criteria which
would be accepted as defining psychological survival, health, well-
being, and their opposites. The selection of these particular criteria
undoubtedly reflected my own values concerning what constitutes a
psychological casualty; they were not, however, idiosyncratic, and at
least in regard to the anti-social category, were shared by the
Leandra group itself. Key informants provided the criteria for substance abuse and for the behaviour which would define a tsotsi and
comtsotsi. Their use thus seemed legitimate in context.

Mediating variables

Clearly, the assessment of the effects on children of trauma is a
complex endeavour. Subject variables, situational variables and
broad contextual factors all interact to produce a particular
response, in a particular person, at any particular moment in time.
However, despite inconsistencies in international research findings,
it does seem that common response patterns may be identified.
Many children and youth do manifest psychological distress in the
face of war and all that it brings. However, this distress may be
short-lived and not necessarily permanently damaging. As in the
case of exposure to general adversity, if youths have adult and community support during and after the trauma occasioned by war, they
are likely to recover relatively quickly. If resources which facilitate
mastery and a sense of self-efficacy are made available to them, this
too facilitates coping.

One of the most important variables which has been shown to
mediate the impact of stress on children and adolescents is the
response of the adult community both at the time of the disaster
and immediately following it. Research on children in World War
Two, and on children exposed to floods, bushfires, tornadoes and
other disasters, all unequivocally indicate that the degree of distress

evidenced is crucially dependent on the responses of the adults in their environment, most especially their parents. When adults provide role models of competence and fearlessness, the children are far less adversely affected than when parents do not cope. Children who are separated from their parents or from familiar adult support show the most acute distress reactions in situations of disaster.

In the Leandra group the importance of parents and adult figures as mediators of stress was inescapable. In their descriptions of the uprisings in the townships, the appeal to adult and community figures for reassurance was clear. Individuals who managed to retain strong family ties both in everyday life and through times of disaster were most resilient. This applied to both the leaders and the followers. Leaders who were not supported in their activities by their families were very vulnerable. Those who had intense ties to their families, but were involved in conflicts of loyalty between their political and personal commitments, fared worst of all. The substratum of resilience laid down in their early years through their intense attachment to parental figures seemed severely corroded by this later conflict.

In fact, one of the single most important factors which distinguished the leaders from the followers was the nature of the political socialisation and support they had received from significant adults. The leaders, far more than any others in the group, had a history of resistance in their families. Some of the followers had parents who were supportive of their participation in the struggle, but very few had parents with a history of resistance. The leaders were therefore inducted into the struggle by different processes than others in the group. Their values were learned in the intimacy of the home. They were taught directly and role models were immediately available. They were not inducted primarily by the peer group, as were many of the others. Because they were more often inducted into the struggle by others in their extended family, the consisten leaders more often had access to continuous support for their activ ties than those who were followers. Youths whose parents did n support their activities, or even actively opposed them, were mu more vulnerable both to dropping out and to becoming criminalis

In summary, the research findings on the whole support the no that young people are potentially resilient and that given the op tunity to heal, they do. This does not mean that they are unaff by their experiences; it simply means they have the capacity to

being overwhelmed by them in the long term. However, this capacity to recover is crucially dependent upon the provision of a benign environment in the post-trauma phase. A benign environment was precisely what was lacking for many of the Leandra youth, and the high casualty figure of 50 per cent is not therefore surprising.

In the wake of their traumatic experiences in 1986, the Leandra group continued to face the severe adversity that had been their lot prior to 1986. Conflict in the township persisted and certainly the material hardships that many of them endured did not abate. Most of the Leandra youth went home not to benign environments, but to situations which may even have deteriorated in their absence. Many had to drop out of school and very few could find employment. At the time of follow-up only 45 per cent of the original group were still in school. Of those who had dropped out only two had succeeded in finding jobs. It was perhaps the extremity of the hardships endured by the Leandra youth and thousands of others like them which prompted concern among human rights activists and professional groups about the future of this generation.

Although the effects of passively suffering violence have been relatively well documented, the effects on the psyche of actively participating in violence have been relatively neglected. The most substantial body of literature in the area is that which was compiled in the wake of the Vietnam War. These studies, while they clearly have a bearing on the issue at hand, were conducted in a very different context. On the whole, the extremely negative effects of participation in violence reported by Vietnam veterans were not noted in the same degree and intensity in the Leandra group. This seeming lack of distress was noted by human rights activists and the press, and gave rise to questions concerning the potential brutalisation of this generation. Because this question was raised frequently during 1984–86, and because of its importance for the future, the following two chapters will explore the Leandra group's relationship to violence and the potential impact of participation in violence upon them.

4 Does Violence Beget Violence?

The high level of violence in the Leandra group is obvious, but the meaning and significance of this, as well as its implications for the future, are not. Are these levels of violence likely to persist, regardless of the circumstances? Or are they likely to abate if the extreme and abnormal situational pressures are to be eased?

The youth who fled Leandra were first seen by the counselling team in 1986 immediately after a series of highly traumatic events. Given the variety and intensity of trauma this group had sustained, it was not surprising that almost everyone in it manifested some signs of psychological disturbance. Apart from their individual effects, these traumatic events severely affected the life of the group as a whole, resulting in episodes of violence which led to the perception of the youngsters as violent and uncontained. These events, however, need to be understood within the context of the developmental stages and group processes described below.

All the individuals in the group were between twelve and twenty-two years; they spanned early to late adolescence, traditionally a time of conflict between conformity and rebellion, dependence and independence, although the degree and nature of such conflicts varies in different cultures. These variations and the notion of adolescence itself are culture-bound, and the degree to which conventional psychological literature is applicable to black township youths is clearly open to debate. Yet many of the observations regarding adolescents in the West, especially their conflicts with conventional authority figures, do seem applicable. However, in the Leandra group, these developmental conflicts were intensified by their interaction with predictable group processes springing from the social and political context.

In our discussion of research on group processes, Freud (1921) serves as a starting-point, as he was one of the first social scientists who endeavoured to understand what he considered to be the infantile or regressive behaviour of groups. In his paper 'Group Psychology and the Analysis of the Ego' (1921), he attempted to explain this phenomenon by pointing to the ambivalence toward authority figures experienced by individuals in the Oedipal position. He believed this ambivalence was re-evoked in groups. By postulating that group members relate to the leader as the primal father, Freud sought to explain the extreme obedience of individuals in groups, which facilitates their mobilisation toward both destructive and altruistic behaviour.

Wilfred Bion (1961) elaborated upon this notion of ambivalence and highlighted the characteristic modes of dealing with ambivalence towards authority figures which evolve in groups. He described three basic assumptions or stances toward the world that develop: dependency, fight–flight, and pairing. In the dependency assumption, the group idealises the leader as an omnipotent, omniscient figure who will provide protection, nurturance and security. There is an expectation that dependency needs will be met. Passivity is the primary mode of being in this stage, and remains dominant until it becomes clear that the leader cannot totally fulfil these needs. At this point disappointment and hostility set in. Revolutions are planned and the leader is frequently deposed, and a new one sought.

In the fight–flight assumption, the basic aim is not dependency but preservation. The group experiences a sense of threat. The leader is called upon to mobilise it as if for attack or flight. In this phase the group acts out or avoids emotions rather than attempting to symbolise or experience them directly. Emotions commonly acted out are rage, sacrifice and martyrdom (Munich & Astrachan, 1983). Emotions of vulnerability, pain and dependence are avoided and denied.

In the pairing assumption, the aim of the group is reproduction. Pairing is an antidote to contemplating issues of termination and separation. Once again vulnerability, pain and dependence are avoided, but through different methods to those used in the fight–flight assumption. Hope and optimism are the emotions which underpin the pairing assumption, and acting out is sexual in nature.

From Bion's perspective, all these assumptions serve to maintain a split between positive and negative emotions. To bring these feelings together and experience them within a single psyche creates too much distress. Projection of emotion onto the leader, group members and outsiders is therefore a common phenomenon, regardless of the assumption within which the group operates. Heroes, scapegoats, earth-mothers and wise old men are sought to embody the hopes and fears of the group.

That groups do indeed encompass these basic assumptions was confirmed by Philip Slater (1966), following a number of longitudinal studies on naturally occurring groups (Munich & Astrachan, 1983). Slater's primary concern is with the evolution of religious structures in groups. His starting-point on a macroscopic level is the silence of the deities, which he believes activates a particular group process. Slater, like Bion, believes that the silence of the deities, like the silence of the leader, is experienced by the group as a deprivation and frustration of their desire for authority and direction. It is also experienced as severe deprivation of the basic human need for nurturance. Following the failure of the leader or the deities to provide nurturance and direction, revolt becomes inevitable. In this phase, themes of murder and sacrifice become common. The leader must die so the group can live. The deities must be obliterated. Intergroup cohesion and unity is heightened as individuals combine forces against the common enemy, and the group moves into the stage parallel to Bion's fight–flight assumption.

Following the deposition of the leader and occasioned by it, there emerges a stage of heightened sexuality among group members corresponding to Bion's basic assumption of pairing. In stressing the active role of women in this phase of revolt, Slater departs from Freud (1913), who in *Totem and Taboo* hypothesised a more passive and withdrawn role for them. However, the parallels between Slater's, Bion's and Freud's observations are striking, and these observations proved invaluable in attempting to understand the events that occurred at Wilgespruit.

The Leandra group was in a state of disarray when it arrived. It had been subjected to a number of traumas, including the death of a father figure. It was thus leaderless and bereft. Group members had been directed to Wilgespruit by trusted authority figures. Their expectations were that Wilgespruit would provide them with shelter, protection and nurturance, authority and guidance. Thus the circumstances of their arrival predisposed group members to Bion's basic assumption of dependency.

The degree of their trauma and their dislocation had led in fact to a massive stimulation of needs for authoritative direction and nurturance. Hope for the satisfaction of these needs would naturally have been invested in the staff at Wilgespruit, who initially would have been automatically cast into the role of omniscient, omnipotent protectors. Against the backdrop of these expectations and fantasies, the reality group members confronted was a stark one. On a physical level they were indeed given shelter, food and protection, but on a psychic level they were left without direction and without special care or nurturance.

The Wilgespruit staff themselves had not been prepared for the arrival of the group; their main focus was on providing physical care for this large number of people who had arrived unexpectedly. Furthermore, they expected this group to stay at the centre for two to three days only. They therefore did not see themselves as being required to engage therapeutically with its members. Besides, there was a language barrier as only a few of the youth spoke English and very few of the staff could communicate in an African language. For all these reasons the staff came to appear as Slater's obstinate, withholding, silent deities or authorities.

In any group, this situation would have been enough to provoke a sharp reaction and would have been sufficient to initiate the rebellion and revolt of Bion's (1961) fight–flight assumption. There was nothing remarkable, therefore, about the fact that at Wilgespruit group rebellion ensued. It is the intensity and organised nature of this rebellion that demands comment, as do the specific events which triggered off its particularly intense manifestations.

The food boycott, for example, occurred shortly after the group arrived. In the individual interviews, both at the time of the boycott and three years later, several issues emerged as triggers of this reaction. Firstly, the food was perceived to be unpalatable, largely because it was unfamiliar. Many of the group spoke of the porridge as being 'liquid and runny rather than firm and stiff'. It was also made of 'oats rather than mielies or corn'. A second issue mentioned by a large number of the youths as a source of discontent was the fact that they were the last to eat. The different groups who had hired Wilgespruit to host their workshops and programmes were fed first, and this the Leandra group resented. A third issue was dislike of the kitchen staff, who the group felt reciprocated this dislike on ideological grounds, as the staff were members of AZAPO.

Even a superficial analysis of these issues reveals their symbolic significance. Complaints about the alien quality of the food were clearly representative of the group's sense of dislocation from its roots, its relocation in a strange environment. The fact that food rather than anything else became the focus of this feeling of dislocation was also to be expected. Food, as the most basic of human requirements, has a universal symbolic significance in relation to nurturance, caring and hospitality, and it is very commonly used to express a variety of emotions, including resentment.

All infants' initial contacts with their new extra-uterine environment are through food. How adequately the baby's needs for food and drink are met influences the basic sense of trust or mistrust that the individual develops. The provision of adequate food in the correct amounts and at the appropriate times is highly determinant of the individual's sense of well-being in the new, frightening and chaotic environment into which he or she has been precipitated. Subsequent experiences of dislocation and relocation, particularly under conditions of extreme trauma, resonate with the infant's early experience of being expelled into a frightening and chaotic world. They reactivate heightened needs around orality and there is a stimulation of deep fears and feelings of mistrust, which frequently express themselves in relation to food and nurturance.

Raphael (1986), in her work on disaster psychiatry, comments specifically on the experience of dislocation and relocation, and notes how common it is for groups in exile to be antagonistic to their new environments. There is an idealisation of the old world and a denigration of the new. She notes further that it is very common for this antagonism to be expressed around basic human needs concerned with food, cooking, toilet and ablution facilities, because trauma fosters regression and so reactivates early anxieties around basic needs. Early developmental anxieties, particularly in regard to dependence, are stimulated, and with this the resentment that dependence can breed is also re-evoked. The reawakening of these early resentments accounts for the antagonism refugees frequently feel towards their new environment.

An alternative explanation for the aggression that is commonly unleashed in these situations around such basic issues is provided by Freud (1913). In *Totem and Taboo* he stresses the importance of social taboos in containing and controlling basic drives, including aggression. While taboos serve to contain aggression, their transgression serves to unleash it. Taboos that develop around food pertain not only to what may or may not be eaten, where and when eating takes place, but also to who may be served first or last. The sequence in which people are served often acts as a marker of status. Men, older or more important people are served in a particular order. Failure to observe the norms and rituals around food which are indigenous to a particular group, even though these norms may not have the status of a taboo, can easily be experienced as highly insulting. Norms and rituals frequently serve to mark the boundaries of a group and define who is an insider and who is a stranger or outcast. The group at Wilgespruit clearly experienced being the last to be fed as an insult and as a hostile act on the part of the staff. They were in reality strangers at the centre, and these actions emphasised their status.

The staff were completely unaware of these dynamics. From their perspective, the group had been willingly accommodated and catered for at extremely short notice. They were not aware of the degree to which the youngsters felt traumatised. They were also unaware of the degree to which these feelings were unacceptable to the youths themselves, given their perception of themselves as free-dom fighters. As a self-defined force of liberation they believed they should be brave, independent and assertive. Direct expression of vulnerability was not allowed, and was experienced as deeply threatening to the identity of both individuals and the group. Yet emotions were running very high and demanded some form of dis-charge. Acting on these emotions rather than engaging with the pain was clearly an easier psychic option, given the situation.

The distress and anger acted out at Wilgespruit has already been described. This acting out was intense and its violent elements can-not be denied. However, in assessing its significance for the future, one must bear in mind that it occurred against the backdrop of extraordinarily traumatic events. The atmosphere in the township immediately preceding the group's flight was one of aggression and confrontation. The group's identity in context was bound up with their definition of themselves as people in conflict, in opposition both to the state and to vigilantes. In order to express this opposi-tion they had participated in public violence, stay-aways, boycotts and innumerable protest meetings.

The fact therefore that the Leandra group chose to express their distress and discontent at Wilgespruit through what appeared to be rather extreme means, becomes understandable. Their style of protest reflected not only the intensity of their emotions but a form of resistance with which they were familiar. The food boycott, for example, embodied a collective strategy of protest that they had used many times before in the home situation. Boycotts and stay-aways were forms of protest they had learned, and they identified with them as tools of the struggle. Returning to these strategies of protest not only allowed for the expression of accumulated feelings, but allowed the group to recreate a mode of being in the world that was familiar and helped them feel safe. The subsequent election of group members to committees so as to represent their interests to the authorities was also an institutional form which they knew well. The familiarity and the sense of effectiveness they felt while engaged in this form of protest gave them comfort and relief from their real feelings of helplessness and powerlessness.

The ability to take control of one's environment even in small ways has a well-documented salutary effect even in the most devastating circumstances. Traumatised individuals especially need to re-establish a feeling that they can exercise some mastery in the face of events which have overwhelmed them. This is precisely what the Leandra group tried to do.

The intimidation by the group of one of the kitchen staff and their intense verbal assault on one of the counsellors can be seen in some ways as an extension of this need to assert mastery. It can also be seen in terms of the group processes already described, which interacted with various structural problems at Wilgespruit to produce the ensuing level of conflict. Both the attack on the kitchen staff member and that on the counsellor occurred at a particular stage in the life of the group: they were still in the phase of rebellion which had been partially triggered by the abstinent leader syndrome. Furthermore, the particular individuals attacked in these incidents were not chosen fortuitously.

Both instances took place shortly after the group's release from jail into the safekeeping of Wilgespruit. They occurred therefore at a time when there was suspicion and anxiety with regard to the community centre, as well as intense disappointment at its failure to protect them. The fact that Wilgespruit was officially appointed by the state, through the court, as a guardian of the group created a great deal of confusion. Only weeks earlier they had been engaged in acts of public violence against community councillors and anyone associated with the state. Now that Wilgespruit had been officially sanctioned by the courts to serve as a refuge created questions for the group about Wilgespruit's actual relationship with the state. Explanations of judicial procedures did not help to allay their anxiety. The judiciary, like all other legal bodies, was seen to be allied with the state.

It was into this conflict-torn situation that the counselling team was invited by the sanctuary centre staff. The concept of therapy was foreign to the group members, most of whom had never encountered a psychologist. The idea of a 'talking cure' had to be explained to them, as had the idea that people could be emotionally and psychologically wounded as well as physically hurt. The counsellors were aware that this lack of familiarity with the parameters of therapy could create suspicion, especially given the sensitivity of the situation. In context, the implicit injunction in psychotherapy to disclose material about oneself and one's actions lent itself to a misinterpretation of motives.

In order to overcome any suspicion that might have been created, most of the counsellors were initially introduced to the group by community leaders who were already well known and trusted by the group. The youth were reassured that the counsellors were all opposed to apartheid and were sympathetic to the struggle. This went a long way toward establishing their credentials, and a co-operative relationship between the group and the counselling team was established. This situation, however, did not pertain to the counsellor who was subsequently attacked verbally and accused of being a spy. She joined the team after the initial contacts had already been made and was therefore not personally introduced by a community leader. When she arrived to see the group she was not accompanied by anyone the group knew and trusted.

That this happened reflected the initial naiveté of the counselling team, which was composed of middle-class, mainly white mental health professionals who, it rapidly became clear, were unversed in the dynamics of township politics. Most of us had treated ex-detainees and were therefore well aware of the brutality of the state, but we were not familiar with street politics and were out of touch with the lives and daily existence of township activists. Living in peaceful suburbia, the idea of a civil war taking place fifteen kilometres from where we lived had not fully penetrated our consciousness. The knowledge was too powerful, and we also had a clear psychic investment in not fully acknowledging the horror of the situation around us. In consequence of this naiveté and psychic resistance, we made fundamental errors which unnecessarily complicated the relationship between staff and youths.

There were further factors which made the group's relationship to the Wilgespruit staff problematic. One of these pertained to differences in the ideological position of the Leandra group and some of the Wilgespruit staff. The youth identified with the UDF, while many of the staff at Wilgespruit were identified with AZAPO. The youths showed little understanding of the intellectual and strategic differences between these organisations, but they were aware of the antagonism, and having just fled intergroup conflict, albeit of a different order, were particularly sensitive to such differences.

The group's sensitivity to ideological conflicts, as well as their dissatisfactions around food, combined to produce a particular antagonism to one of the kitchen staff, a member of AZAPO. As the person who interacted most directly with the group around the conflictual issues of food preparation and the time of meals, she was held responsible for their dissatisfactions in this area.

This staff member was not psychologically sophisticated; she expected the youth to show gratitude and respect, which she felt was her due as an older person. She communicated her expectations, together with her feeling that the group should show some appreciation of the service rendered by the centre. They retaliated by pointing out that their stay was subsidised by the SACC, and accused the staff in general and this member in particular of making a profit out of them, and of keeping back 'the people's money' for gain.

This perception that the 'people's money' was being abused was a common one in the townships during 1984–86. The accusations need therefore to be seen in this context. Many of the youths, before their flight, had been involved in attacks on local councillors who themselves were victims of the state's policies in that they were expected as a formal body to provide essential services for the townships without state finance. The local councils were expected to be autonomous and self-financing with no real resources other than those generated by licensing fees, house rentals and service charges. They were perceived by the community to be puppets of the state. Any attempt on their part to raise rents was resisted and was seen as an indication that the councillors were feathering their own nests at the expense of the community. The community councils therefore were both politically unpopular and economically unviable (Haysom, 1986). Corruption was rife in many townships, but even when it was not, the impossibility of the situation that councillors faced fostered this perception and deepened the anger of the community against them.

When the group of youth began to believe that money provided for their maintenance at Wilgespruit was not being made available to them, they resorted to the same tactics of intimidation and harassment that they had used against the township councillors.

It has already been noted that the Leandra group had originally constituted itself in conflict. The *raison d'être* for its existence was to enter into confrontation and to challenge perceived injustices in the township. As such it did not have a strong internal cohesion based on shared objectives, beyond the principle of opposition. It was not well organised and in this respect it was not different from many other student and youth groupings of the time. The members were united only by their age, their militancy and the trauma they had endured, and not by a great deal else. To maintain a spirit of militancy was therefore a pillar of unity; the need to preserve themselves as a group was a primary concern. In this preoccupation they shared the concern of all groups who enter the fight–flight assumption described by Bion (1961). In the Leandra group this assumption was magnified, as in its immediate past the group had indeed been engaged in very real fight–flight activities. Thus the assumption took on a particular intensity which informed the group's need to seek out and attack targets at Wilgespruit.

The basic fight–flight assumption of the Leandra group, which was its initial concern, only started to transform itself once the group began to confront its own disintegration. As their stay at Wilgespruit became extended, the group's original *raison d'être* disappeared and the group had to examine its own existence apart from its original context. The net result was that the cohesion of the group began to break down as the need to unite against the common enemy receded. At this point, as might have been predicted by Bion, pairing emerged as the basic group assumption. Heightened sexuality was evoked and acted out, in sharp contrast to the tight discipline the group had exercised over the expression of sexuality on their arrival at Wilgespruit. In these early days, it will be remembered, one of the complaints of the group was that males and females were housed in the same building. As this initial anxiety dissipated, the group retreated from the fight–flight assumption and moved into pairing.

The acting out of sexual impulses created conflict between group members and the staff, who felt responsible for their well-being. It also, as might have been predicted, created intra-group tensions. Personal power struggles emerged, and the group broke into factions as individuals began to assert their own needs more independently of group interests. These rifts were fuelled by the departure of some of the leaders to safer quarters and the arrival of new members from other townships. They were also fuelled by the monotony and boredom of the days at Wilgespruit. The centre was not geared to accommodate youths in the long term. There were no educational facilities and the daily programme, if organised at all, could only be done so on an *ad hoc* basis.

Conflicts developed between those who wished to maintain the group as an integrated unit of freedom fighters, and those who felt the time should be used to relax and replenish their resources. The former sub-group were mindful of the situation at home, to which they wished to return. Many of the people in this sub-group had been in leadership positions on the executives of youth congresses and students representative councils. The alternate group, which felt the time should be used for relaxation and recuperation, vehemently challenged the authority of these leaders and their attempts to enforce discipline. This alternate group included a number of individuals who smoked marijuana, were promiscuous, and who were identified by staff members as having had the most difficulty conforming to the very few rules laid down by the Wilgespruit institution. They were also seen as having the greatest sense of entitlement to privileges and material goods. In other words, they comprised a more anti-social, delinquent group. Clearly though, the breakdown and composition of the two sub-groups was not clear-cut. There were overlaps between the two.

The conflict between some of the marijuana-smokers and the leadership eventually erupted into skirmishes in which members of both groups assaulted each other. This necessitated the intervention of the staff and, as may have been anticipated, led to a closing of the group's ranks once more, as an external enemy could now once again be clearly identified. This situation contributed considerably to deterioration in the relationship between the group and members of staff, some of whom felt very threatened by the extremely aggressive mood of the youths. So aggressive was the mood that a few staff members chose to leave Wilgespruit temporarily.

In retrospect, the dynamics at the interface of the group and the centre are understandable. However, at the time, the events at Wilgespruit and in the country were so new and so momentous that we ourselves were overwhelmed by them. Thus we failed to understand the processes which were operative at the time and so failed to intervene effectively.

As counsellors, we were initially divided in our views on what approach should be adopted. This confusion sprang from different understandings of the situation. Some counsellors related to the youth in terms of their age and the trauma they had sustained; their instinct was to be protective and to provide a safe environment where healing could take place. Others related to the group more in terms of their self-defined identity as freedom fighters and stressed the reality of their lives back in the community. Both positions were passionately defended. The counsellors who emphasised the trauma of the youth felt that to return them prematurely was virtually to pass them on as cannon-fodder. Those who emphasised their status as freedom fighters felt that Wilgespruit was creating a sense of false security and breaking down defences. They felt that this would have negative consequences in the long term, not only in regard to their psychological integration, but also in terms of their participation in the broader political struggle. The viewpoints of both parties were valid, but each implied different strategies for intervention which were not always compatible with each other. This confusion did little to facilitate therapeutic intervention.

In fact this confusion, as well as the overall lack of sensitivity with which the youths were received, probably contributed substantially to the acting-out behaviour that subsequently occurred, as did the general context of violence and trauma in which the group had been steeped. This is not, however, intended to justify their behaviour. It is simply intended to place it in context and provide indications of how to avoid facilitating such behaviour in future. It is also intended to indicate the degree to which contextual rather than more personal factors could be said to have influenced the levels of violence present in the group. That contextual rather than personal factors were more significant is reflected by the shift in the group members' views of violence between the initial encounter and the follow-up.

At Wilgespruit, when attitudes to violence were first assessed, the group was without exception found to be in a very angry and aggressive frame of mind. Most expressed themselves in favour of violent change. This view was informed not only by their belief that real change was impossible without violence, but also by more personal desires for revenge, which at the time were very close to the surface. Nearly all members of the group expressed a desire to hit back at their oppressors and to redress the injustice and trauma to which they had been subjected.

While the revenge motif was shared by most, the targets from whom they wished to exact revenge varied. Individuals differed in terms of whom they held primarily responsible for the current predicament. Some were less preoccupied than others with the origins of their immediate and most recent problems. They saw them in a particular context. They blamed state policies for their plight and wanted to take their revenge against agents of the state. Others blamed whites in general and wished to exact retribution from them. Yet others were preoccupied with more recent events in Leandra and wished to take revenge against the vigilantes and their supporters. Regardless of the target chosen for attack, the revenge fantasies of all members of the group were very violent. Some might have confirmed the worst nightmares of fearful whites. There were expressions of a desire to hurt white children so that 'their parents could feel the pain that black parents feel' as well as a desire to attack white homes. The notion that white suburbia should be shaken out of complacency was commonly articulated. To take the struggle to the white streets was a frequently expressed sentiment.

These fantasies and sentiments need, however, to be seen within their context. All the group members were adolescents, which is a time when fantasies of aggression are common. Given their exposure to violence, however, these fantasies were informed by knowledge rather than innocence. Be this as it may, the importance of trauma in generating fantasies encompassing a high level of violence and a desire for revenge was clear at the time of follow-up; during 1989 a substantial reduction in these fantasies was noted.

The impact of combat and war on adolescent fantasies has been well documented. Working with veterans, Ulman and Brothers (1988) analysed the effects of combat on aggressive fantasies in male adolescents. The particular group they studied were American soldiers of a similar age to the Leandra group at the time of follow-up. Their research focused on the impact of combat on the adolescent's developing sense of self. In agreement with Anna Freud (1958), they spoke of the normal resurgence during adolescence of magical thinking and of feelings of omnipotence.

In times of peace these adolescent fantasies are contained and channelled into forms of expression which limit and moderate them. The common fantasy of 'saving the world', for example, may be expressed through occupational choices such as nursing, social work, or psychology. Similarly, fantasies of power may be expressed through occupational choices, competitive games, participation in student politics, and so on. In times of war, however, society does not contain and modulate these fantasies. In fact, it provides a context which exacerbates them. Soldiers, liberation fighters, defenders of the nation, perceive themselves as saviours of their people, and real opportunities for unlimited power over people frequently present themselves. However, the converse also obtains, and wars may also confront the adolescent with the fact that others may have absolute power over him, and that he may be placed in a helpless, life-threatening position.

Conditions of war therefore expose the adolescent both to the inflation of natural narcissistic fantasies and to their sudden, traumatic deflation. The former predisposes adolescents to the expression and acting out of these fantasies in reality. The latter predisposes them to narcissistic wounds and injuries resulting in feelings of rage and deeply felt desires for revenge (Ulman & Brothers, 1988). In the Leandra group both the acting out of aggression and the desire for revenge were clearly seen.

At the point at which the group's views on violence were originally tapped in 1986, not only was the war ethic in the ascendant, giving social sanction to the expression of views and emotions appropriate to this, but the group was highly traumatised. They were thus in a phase of narcissistic injury, which in itself provokes intense rage and fantasies of revenge. The romanticisation of violence which was undoubtedly present, and the intensity of their revenge fantasies, should be seen in this context. Their attitudes confirm the idea that highly traumatised individuals operating within a war mentality relate to violence as a form of self-defence and as a channel for revenge. How this will affect behaviour in peacetime will depend on many variables other than the simple fact of participation in violence. Certainly, many of the Leandra group had actively participated in violence both before and after their Wilgespruit sojourn; however, as has been pointed out in the case-studies, relatively few became chronically anti-social.

Although 1989 can hardly be regarded as a time of peace, it was a year of far less open conflict in South Africa, not only in Leandra, but across the nation. Massive repression still obtained, but its more violent manifestations on the street were largely absent, except in the latter part of the year when the national elections took place.

By then, most members of the Leandra group were reintegrated into the community. A considerable time had elapsed since their exposure to the more dramatic forms of trauma which characterised their lives in 1984–86. The troops were out of the townships, although their presence in the form of the 'green beans' or municipal police was still felt. Resistance, in line with the state's retreat from the open use of the Defence Force, took a less overtly militant form. The reduction in exposure to trauma allowed some group members to relinquish the fantasies of revenge, and contributed to a reduction in the levels of violence in the fantasies of the group in 1989.

There was far greater diversity of response in the group's attitude to violence in general in 1989. Some had renounced violence altogether. This sub-group felt that it had been counterproductive at both strategic and personal levels. On the strategic plane it was felt that state response to black violence had led to intensified suffering for the black community, with very little gain. In reflecting upon their own participation in violence, they likewise concluded that it had been fruitless. They regretted that they had been carried away on the wave of the group mood; they felt they had lost their own capacity for individual choice and that their humanity had suffered. They rejected violence on principle as a result of this experience. This radical shift in perspective is noteworthy. It indicates clearly the flexibility of human beings, the capacity to reflect upon experience, the ability to move between war and peacetime moralities. Reciprocally, the fact that this group participated in violence at various points in their lives, despite their bias against it, indicates the extent to which group moods and social contexts can influence the individual.

This bias against violence was a minority position in the Leandra group even in 1989. A 90 per cent majority was still in favour of violence, but there was great diversity in how this was conceptualised and what gains it was believed would result. A small minority focused on personal gain and the revenge motif, both in relation to the vigilantes and to whites. The members of this group were not discriminating in their attitudes. They saw all whites as the enemy. They spoke of 'showing the whites that blacks are not cowards' and of 'making the Boers feel pain too'. They felt that attacking civilian targets was acceptable even if so-called 'innocent whites die because whites are not innocent', civilian or otherwise. Comments such as these were reminiscent of those made by the majority in 1986.

A more common position stressed that violence had no value in itself but did have a strategic value in the armed struggle. This position emphasised the importance of restraint and discipline. Individuals advocating this position were strongly against exacting personal revenge. They stressed strategic value. They believed in strikes against hard targets, such as police stations and military bases, but were on the whole against strikes at civilian targets. They argued that, strategically speaking, it would lead to a loss of support from sympathetic whites and would allow the state to stir up paranoia and security fever; they also expressed ethical considerations about the loss of innocent lives. The few individuals in this group who still supported attacks on soft targets, unlike those in the revenge group, justified strikes against civilians purely in strategic terms. The death of civilians, they felt, would lead the white constituency to intensify its pressure on the state to take black grievances seriously and to work toward some solution of the country's problems. This sub-group did not classify all whites as the enemy. It was aware of the conflicts and tensions amongst whites, and did not characterise them in monolithic terms.

This diversity of response and the diminishing hold of the revenge motif indicates the degree to which the situation, rather than the personalities of individuals, created the high levels of aggression present in their fantasies in 1986. All the same, it is doubtful that the experience of being a victim or a perpetrator of violence leaves no scars at all. While in 1989 only 10 per cent of the group were classified as tsotsis or comtsotsis in the sense that they were involved in anti-social activities, a further 40 per cent showed sufficient signs of distress to be classified as psychological casualties in terms of other dimensions. It is impossible to determine whether this was directly related to their exposure to violence or was the result of living in more general conditions of adversity.

When the responses of individuals to participation in violence were probed, there was little uniformity. Subtle differences emerged, especially in regard to participation in its more severe forms. In the context of less severe violence, there was greater uniformity of response. Very few reported being disturbed by their participation in attacks on property. Almost everyone reported that during the attacks they were caught up in the mood of the crowd. Most felt anger and elation; only a few felt fear. Similarly, after the event most people reported feeling empowered by the experience: they were acting to change their situation rather than passively accepting it, with positive emotional effects. However, this positive value frequently was lost after the crowd dispersed.

When individuals were once more alone, many reported a mixture of fear and emptiness in the immediate aftermath. They felt suddenly overwhelmed by the enormity of what they had done. There was an awareness that some internal control had been breached; the disturbed awareness that a sacred cow had been killed seeped into the individual consciousness. It was a feeling that seemed difficult to admit to, as acknowledging it felt like a betrayal of group solidarity.

Fast on the heels of this awe at the breach of internal controls came the fear of reprisal. All members of the group reported their fear of being attacked by vigilantes, or detained. This persisted for several days. During this phase they found comfort in the degree to which the experience was a shared one, which offered some degree of protection and anonymity. It also allowed individuals to discuss their fears and to find support.

Furthermore, many found reassurance in the fact that adults and community leaders had been involved in these events too. They felt that this lent a moral legitimacy to their actions. In this admission the need of youth for adult models was once more revealed. So was the need to maintain a sense of morality in the midst of events which broke with conventional views of right and wrong; in the immediate aftermath of the violence there was clearly a need to reassert restraint and order.

Adult models during this time provided support and the possibility of protection from outside attacks. They also provided justification for the events and moral reassurance. This does not mean that adults and community leaders always approved of the activities of the youths. This, as we have seen, was certainly not the case. Youth were often felt to indulge in excesses, and there was a perceived need to hold them in check, to hold them accountable for their actions. However, when there were incidents of joint mass action in the township, as when councillors' houses were attacked, the youth drew support and strength from their elders as well as reassurance about the morality of their actions. The validity of their struggle for equality and justice within the context of war was reaffirmed.

The need to affirm the validity and legitimacy of violent action was even stronger, as were the negative effects of participation, when attacks involved persons and not only property. However, these negative consequences, whether in the form of clinical symptomatology or persistent anti-social behaviour, did not seem to be inevitable; once again it depended upon contextual variables.

Approximately 80 per cent of the sub-group interviewed at the time of follow-up had either witnessed or been involved in attacks on a person construed as an enemy. Approximately 30 per cent of this sub-group reported being very negatively affected by it, while the others did not. Among this 30 per cent were individuals who reported being very negatively affected, even if they did not actually participate in violence, but only failed to intervene to prevent it.

The factors which determined whether or not persons were affected by their participation in violence, both in the Leandra group and in the literature, can be summarised as follows. With regard to the development of clinical symptomatology, the greater the degree of empathy individuals have with their victims, the more distressed they become. That is, the more individuals identify with the victim, perceive the victim as similar to the self and imagine the self in a similar predicament, the greater their distress. The more gruesome the act, the greater the negative consequences reported. The more individuals feel an act of violence has been committed in a state of frenzy, the greater the negative impact. Conversely, the more they believe an act of violence is necessary within the context of transcendent values, such as the notion of a just war, the better they are able to deal with it. In sum, the less guilty they feel about the act, the less distressed they are.

The capacity to experience empathy and guilt is crucial to the survival of humaneness and compassion. To destroy these capacities is to destroy the humanity of the individual and to produce a brutalised person. It is difficult to assess what kind of impact participation in the political violence of 1984–86 had upon the capacity for empathy and guilt of township youths. Certainly for the majority of the Leandra group, these events did seem to affect their experience of empathy and guilt. However, it did not seem that these capacities were destroyed in a general sense. Instead, the events of 1984–86 acted to define rather precisely the limits of human sympathy and to demarcate clearly those for whom it was appropriate or inappropriate to experience empathy. The majority of the Leandra group reported a sense of heightened empathy with those they would define as insiders and a lessening of it in relation to outsiders. Thus their exposure to political violence, while it inhibited empathy in one context, enhanced it in others. Given the relationship between empathy and violence, namely that empathy acts to inhibit violence, it would be fair to conclude that there was not a general disinhibition of aggression in the majority of these youth. There was rather disinhibition of aggression in particular contexts and a reciprocal inhibition of it in others.

In sum, there is little evidence of the Leandra youth having become a brutalised generation in the sense that their capacity for empathy and guilt as such had been impaired. There was similarly little to indicate that they would engage in indiscriminate and arbitrary violence, although there was much to indicate that violence would be their response to particular sets of circumstances. For the majority, although expressions of violence could be stimulated by particular contexts, these expressions still seemed to be contained within strict boundaries and governed by a system of morality which could be observed and articulated. Nevertheless, there was a minority whose behaviour was not bound in this way and who were given to violent outbursts of an indiscriminate and arbitrary nature. The case history of Silas and Len (see Chapter 3) provides examples of two such individuals.

In reading Len's case history, it is clear that he had many personal difficulties which pre-dated his involvement in the struggle. There were few indications, however, that these expressed themselves in overtly anti-social ways prior to 1984–86. It was his participation in the struggle which seemed to open up different avenues for the expression of his deeply felt discontents. It also initially offered him certain psychological satisfactions which, at least in the short term, acted to ameliorate some of his discontent. In the long term, however, his participation in this situation aggravated his difficulties. His assault at the hands of the vigilantes increased the intensity of his frustration and rage, and provoked a strong desire for revenge. This was at first directed quite specifically, but following his fall from grace in the community at large, it became more generalised and indiscriminate.

Len's participation in the struggle not only provoked anger and frustration which needed an outlet, but it also taught him that his frustration could be directly expressed against others. His participation in collective resistance taught him about the power of the group, and he subsequently exploited this power for personal gain. His involvement in public violence reinforced for him the fact that violence has an instrumental value in achieving desired objectives, and it also provided him with a set of justifications for his own behaviour. He clung to the political justifications for violence originally used by the comrades in their resistance to authority, to justify his own subsequent anti-social actions, even though these justifications now lacked any legitimation by the broader community.

Ironically, however, the fact that Len, and individuals like him, need these justifications to legitimate their behaviour offers some hope, for their future.

Individuals like Len show a clear desire to be integrated into a web of intimate interpersonal relationships which can contain them. They show a clear desire to have a purpose and an ideal to which they can commit themselves. Reintegration programmes such as those instituted in Zimbabwe since the civil war, which recognise the need of youth for purpose and meaning as well as affiliation and belonging, are therefore likely to be highly successful with groups of individuals like Len. But they are less likely to be successful with individuals whose anti-social behaviour is less directly linked with political disaffection, and more directly linked with general adversity and the culture of violence this generates.

That slum conditions and general adversity in and of themselves facilitate anti-social behaviour is well established, and certainly the excessive crime rates in South Africa's townships demonstrate this. In fact, the extraordinarily high levels of crime in the townships, and the state's inability or unwillingness to control it, were one of the rallying points for the resistance movement in the first place. The people's courts and the disciplinary committees which were a feature of township life in 1984–86 were attempts by the community to control rampant crime. However, the existence of such a high incidence in the first place is a clear reflection of how appalling township conditions in fact are. Gangs too have always been a feature of township life, but their numbers and the degree to which they have become involved in criminal activity seem to have increased over the last decades (Davis, 1991).

The enormity of the problem is partly due to the fact that the sheer number of people living in townships has increased and there has been a concurrent rise in levels of unemployment and poverty. There has also arisen a general culture of violence which is not specifically related to exposure to political conflict. The diaries of Soweto children, collected by Mtshali (1982) and analysed by Richter (1989), have revealed a shocking level of violence in the everyday life of eight-year-old children, even prior to the escalation of civil conflict. For average Soweto children, nearly every day of their lives is characterised by exposure to some episode of violence in their immediate surroundings.

The most destructive element of this exposure is the degree to which violence is perceived to be part of everyday life. This in itself, if children are not simultaneously exposed to loving, caring relationships in situations of stable child-care, could be sufficient to promote pervasive and indiscriminate anti-social behaviour. This kind of anti-social behaviour is far more difficult to contain than that stimulated by individual experience in civil conflict.

While thus far we have emphasised that it is the exceptional individual rather than the average youth who has become chronically and indiscriminately anti-social, this does not mean that the average youth has been unaffected by exposure either to general adversity or to civil conflict. The degree to which general adversity was the dominant theme in the youths' own narratives was clearly revealed in the case-studies. Furthermore, exposure to civil strife and participation in it did affect many individuals negatively. However, individuals participated in the strife in different ways and were affected to different degrees by it.

One lesson which all those who psychologically survived their involvement in civil strife had to come to grips with, was that the morality appropriate to civilian life is not the same morality appropriate to war. They had to accept that in war the exercise of violence is condoned, while in civilian life it is not. Both the appropriate exercise of violence and its restraint are lessons which all those who have ever engaged in war have had to learn.

The general conclusion to which this study points is that most of the Leandra group learned this. Only 10 per cent of the group at the time of follow-up were thought to be hard-core tsotsis whose general capacity for empathy has been damaged, and whose aggression is exercised with little restraint, mainly for the purpose of economic survival or self-gain. Their aggression is entrenched and requires no self-justification. The other group was thought to comprise youth whose behaviour is indeed anti-social but seems to be less entrenched. They are politically disaffected, but still retain an idealism and a need to justify their behaviour in political terms. All this offers hope for the future. However, this hope for the future is clearly contingent upon providing for the majority of black youth the opportunities for which they have been fighting.

5 Coming to Terms with Violence

Participation in violence in the context of war has been a characteristic of the human condition throughout the ages. In twenty-four centuries of recorded history, European states have, on average, gone to war once every five years. Similarly, since 1945, it has been more common for governments to be replaced through revolution than through elections (Gurr, 1970).

Participation in war and its accompanying violence was until very recently seen as part of a boy's rite of passage to adulthood. In the past, however, it was simply expected that individuals would have the capacity to distinguish a state of war from a state of peace, and that they would behave accordingly on transition from one to the other. What concern there was focused initially on soldiers who were traumatised by war and developed clinical symptoms such as post-traumatic stress disorder, depression and anxiety. The focus was not on its brutalising potential; far more attention was given to the effects of being a victim rather than a perpetrator of violence.

It was only after Vietnam that questions concerning the effects of participation in violence began to be asked on any scale. This questioning coincided with a change in public opinion about the 'legitimacy of war in general and the Vietnam War in particular. Soldiers too have begun to question not only their own involvement in war but also the society that places them in this untenable position. It is perhaps this questioning of war rather than participation as such which has led to the extraordinarily high reported incidence of psychological casualties among returning soldiers. The psychological literature certainly does not indicate that participating in war or perpetrating violence itself automatically leads either to the development of clinical symptomatology or entrenched anti-social behaviour. In fact, there is a body of thought which would indicate the opposite. This literature proposes that under certain circumstances, violence might in fact have positive psychological effects.

The chief proponent of this view, Fanon (1963), together with Freud (1932) and Miller (1983), explored the psychological meaning of the pursuit of violence in the context of war. There were, however, major differences in the three approaches. Miller saw violence as a desperate attempt by persons damaged by authoritarian and repressive child-rearing practices to cure themselves by projecting humiliated parts of themselves onto others and then attacking them. She acknowledged the ameliorative potential of violence for individual distress in the short term, but believed that in the long term it could never really be a healing force. In this she was at odds with Fanon, who saw violence not only as ameliorating distress in the short term, but as an essential aspect of a long-term cure for those who had suffered oppression.

Fanon's starting point is the damage inflicted upon individuals by living in a political system which demeans and exploits them, and which projects onto them all the disowned negative aspects of the oppressor. He speaks of the fury this generates in the oppressed, which of necessity must be repressed and replaced by an outward conformity to the oppressor's dictates. This fury which is denied an outlet may turn in upon itself in self-destruction. Alternatively, it may be directed outward against a scapegoat, which explains the frequency with which the oppressed attack one another, relating to one another in the dehumanised terms that were imposed upon them.

Fanon's analysis of the importance of violence in individual terms is part of a larger argument embracing the strategic importance of violence in uniting the oppressed as a group and in coercing the oppressor as a collective entity. Violence within Fanon's terms is not embraced primarily as an act of the individual warrior-hero. Its value lies not simply in 'slaying the tyrant in his seat of power' and in delivering the masses, but in defining the individual's identity as part of the mass to be delivered, rather than apart from it as an independent saviour. He stresses the importance of the collective because oppression acts to privatise pain, and victimisation acts to deprive the person of family life, community and history. The re-establishment of a sense of community and history by immersion in the collective is therefore vital to psychological liberation.

In contrast to both Miller and Fanon, Freud did not conceptualise participation in violence within the parameters of a response to abuse and oppression. He saw it as part of the repertoire of all human beings, exercised in response to 'normal' rather than especially abusive conditions. Freud believed that man has an active instinct for hatred and destructiveness. This is juxtaposed with an active instinct for self-preservation, the life instinct. Participation in war, or collective violence, allows the sanctioned expression of both instincts. Freud postulated that in small-scale traditional societies, the engagement of these two impulses within the individual was simple and direct. External controls within the society dictated what was good or bad. Its simple organisation allowed for continual monitoring of individual behaviour, and for immediate reward or punishment. There was no real need for individuals to monitor their own behaviour by way of the superego, or conscience; external sanctions were sufficient.

Modern societies, by contrast, cannot monitor individual behaviour in the same way. Their harmony is dependent on individuals monitoring their own behaviour, and for this purpose it is crucial that the individual conscience or superego be fostered. Once this development has been fostered, however, individual action becomes dependent not only upon external sanctions but also upon internal controls. Society is no longer free to mobilise action as directly as it once was.

In mustering the modern person for war, some appeal has to be made to the superego through ideals and transcendent moralities. Some way has to be found for people to justify their action to themselves, because it is necessary for the maintenance of society to place violent actions under some form of internal prohibition.

As Freud (1932) pointed out, it is not difficult for society to devise appeals to ideology which would facilitate such justification at the individual level. However, when a society is itself ambivalent about granting this permission because large sectors of it condemn war, and there is no consistency in the moral prescription put forward, the individual is left in an untenable position. As early as 1919, at the close of World War One, Freud spoke of the difficulties individuals had in integrating the sharply different realities that war and peace encompassed. He indicated that many coped with this disjunction by splitting the ego into a 'peaceful ego' and its parasitic, war-like double. This notion of a split ego resonates with the understanding of many researchers who have subsequently worked with adolescent combatants. Lifton (1973), working in the context of the Vietnam War, spoke of the 'death of the civilian self and its rebirth as a military self' which is numbed and prone to violence. Shatan (1977) argues similarly that adolescent soldiers live with two psychic realities, one pertaining to peace and one to war. These realities are separated by a psychic membrane. If this is penetrated sufficiently to allow the two realities to collide, massive psychological trauma and breakdown occur.

These images are all highly evocative, and experience with the Leandra group indicates that they capture an aspect of the psychic reality of the adolescent in combat. What was different about the Leandra group, however, was the degree to which the youth found themselves in combat in the midst of civilian life. They were not conscripted soldiers within a conventional army fighting battles in a combat zone. Yet they were engaged in what they saw as a civil war, a perception shared by many prominent black leaders, despite the fact that no official war had been declared. There were troops in the townships; there were deaths and injuries sustained in running battles between security forces and the youth; there was armed conflict with competing anti-apartheid groups and vigilantes.

At the same time, the youth were meant to attend school as usual, and to carry on with their daily affairs. The Leandra group could not therefore afford the suspension of their old peacetime egos. They had to maintain both their war and peace egos simultaneously and to integrate them into an overarching identity, if they were to cope with both realities. This was an enormous psychic task which had many implications for their psychological survival.

Furthermore, the situation in the township lent itself to confusion. The usual markers which clearly define a state of war, the identity of an enemy and when it is appropriate to engage in offensive behaviour, were absent. It was very easy to mistake friends for enemies, for example, especially given the state's attempts to foster suspicion and fragmentation in the black community. It was also easy to over-generalise the situations in which aggression was appropriate. When individuals did over-generalise and then realised the mistake they had made, it created psychological distress, and complicated their attempts to integrate their own behaviour into coherent, cohesive identities. Many then judged themselves in terms of values and attitudes appropriate to their peacetime egos and experienced great guilt.

Conversely, others dealt with the situation by not being prepared to acknowledge their mistakes, even when they were blatant. A common response was to justify errors intellectually in the name of the struggle and to invoke the values appropriate to a wartime identity. However, when these justifications were not met with common approval within the community – and they often were not – this also complicated the attempts of individuals to integrate their own behaviour.

These difficulties were compounded by the fact that the youth frequently used similar tactics for bargaining with friends to those they used for bargaining with enemies. Such a failure of differentiation has perhaps contributed to the many spontaneous outbursts of violence that have remained a feature of township life.

These complexities of response have had a price, in terms of both the amount of clinical symptomatology evidenced and the ease with which spontaneous violence (which is not to be confused with indiscriminate violence) can be sparked off.

However problematic these issues might be, the Leandra youth were not without a sense of morality, nor was their capacity for empathy destroyed. In fact, in relation to their comrades, family, and friends, their empathy seems to have been heightened rather than diminished. Nevertheless, it cannot be denied that this increase in empathy for family and friends had been coupled with a hardening of the boundary between groups of individuals for whom it was felt appropriate to have empathy, and those for whom it was not. That this is problematic cannot be denied.

Group membership has always and universally been a factor which has defined the limits within which human sympathy may be expressed. Moralities, including those pertaining to violence, are generally accepted to be reflective of the structure of solidarity groups. They dictate the limits within which empathy is exercised and the boundaries outside of which it is not expected to operate. That is, group membership defines the boundaries outside of which violence may be expressed. Such violence in fact has always been accepted as one means by which groups establish the limits of their identification with those whom they consider worthy of human status and humane treatment (Collins, 1973).

In small-scale societies, the identification of those who were considered human, or like the self, and those who were alien, was relatively simple. Identification occurred along kinship lines and was constrained within certain geographical boundaries. In these societies injunctions against killing extended only to the boundary of the group (Collins, 1973). In modern societies, the identification of solidarity groups is far more complex. Kinship networks have broken down and there are much higher levels of geographic mobility. Societies are more cosmopolitan and offer multiple options for the formation of solidarity groups. There are multiple markers which will determine an individual's identification with others and his or her own identity in turn. An individual's allegiances across the dimensions of race, class, nationality, religion and ideological persuasion may be diverse and may include a large number of people, but each dimension will set a boundary for identification and for moral obligation. The potential within this structure for universal brotherhood does exist, and it is supported ideologically within the major world religions, including Christianity. However, Christianity has also been one of the markers of group membership most consistently used to define the limits of morality and human sympathy (Collins, 1973).

In the Leandra group, Christianity was not one of the primary markers of group membership, nor did it set the boundary of empathy. Race and ideological persuasion were far more important markers. Christianity was more relevant as a factor that influenced superego concerns. Because the majority of the group identified themselves as Christians, they had to grapple very directly with the question of the morality of violence within this framework. A very small minority believed that Christianity should lead to pacifism. Others did not conceptualise the dictates of Christianity in this way. They identified with the tenets of liberation theology, which stresses the obligations on Christians to identify with the poor and to fight for social justice. It does not condone violence, but stresses the need to fight injustice at all costs. Within this framework, violence against an institution which deliberately obstructs the cause of social justice is conceivable, although it is never to be embarked upon lightly. Thus engagement in violence in and of itself need not necessarily constitute a transgression against either the principles of Christianity or the dictates of the superego.

The subtleties and differences in beliefs and in group identifications in the Leandra group had a profound effect on how members of this group were affected by their participation in violence and their witnessing of it, as the following case studies will illustrate. They deal specifically with individuals who were involved in the notorious phenomenon of 'necklacing' and other forms of human burnings which were common between 1984 and 1986.

The incidents of necklacing were so horrifying and numerous – 600 up to 1988 according to the South African Institute of Race Relations (1988) – that the origins and roots of the practice in common social processes have been all but obscured. They were not confined to the urban areas. While in the towns the usual rationale was that the victim was an informer or *impimpi*, in the rural areas witchcraft accusations were common. Wherever the burnings took place, however, similar social processes were involved. The burnings of putative witches and *impimpis* (informers) all occurred in contexts of massive social upheaval and catastrophic community disruption, after traumatic and violent events had threatened the entire community and led to the injury and death of some of its members.

Situations of this nature lend themselves to the experience of what Lifton (1973) has termed 'death-taintedness' – they facilitate atrocities. Working in the context of the Vietnam War, Lifton described atrocity-generating situations in some detail. These are situations in which individuals and communities experience themselves as threatened by ubiquitous forces which cannot be easily identified or attacked. Injury and death can and do strike at any time. The community is relatively powerless in the face of these uncontrollable forces. Fear of death and injury, the powerlessness of the group, and a lack of internal cohesion combine to promote the experience of death-taintedness which underpins the commission of atrocities. As a means of coping with this extremely disturbing experience, the group feels impelled to purge itself. It does so by projecting the quality onto other individuals or groups, and then attacking them in order to destroy the death-taintedness now contained within them.

The parallels between Lifton's thoughts on the death-taintedness of abused groups and Alice Miller's perspective on child abuse are striking. Both see atrocities and abuse as the result of damage and injury inflicted upon the individual or group. Both comment on the psychic functions atrocities serve. Both agree that atrocities are attempts to destroy in the other, humiliated and damaged parts of the self which have been projected onto the other.

Lifton, working at the level of the group, develops these notions further. He points out that victimisation of others is not only an attempt to get rid of negative experiences such as death-taintedness. It serves a purpose beyond this, becoming a perverted attempt by the group to immortalise itself. The group threatened by death seeks at some level to overcome it symbolically by the survival of other deaths, witnessed or perpetrated. The group enters into a 'survivor paranoia'. In this state, it becomes imperative to identify a concrete cause of the problems experienced and then to annihilate this cause. Through this annihilation the group wishes not only to rid the community of threats to its survival, but to affirm the continuity of the community with life. Symbolically overcoming death serves this purpose.

Researchers other than Lifton who have studied atrocities concur that they serve important psychological functions. Shorter (1985), for example, working in the context of medieval witch-burnings, argued that these attacks served several purposes. They provided an explanation for the great misfortunes which had befallen the community, and this explanation in turn created the opportunity to take steps to prevent further mishaps. They also provided an emotional outlet for group emotions as well as an opportunity to exact instant justice.

Shorter stressed that the person attacked is never randomly selected, but is chosen in terms of predictable parameters used in the selection of scapegoats in atrocities of all kinds. The social upheaval in which such atrocities occur acts to undermine structures and hierarchies within the group while, at the same time, external threats solidify clear boundaries between the group and the outside world. In situations characterised by such inner flux and by such clear external threats, strict conformity becomes the yardstick used by communities to distinguish friends from foes. In this context it is the eccentric, the misfit and the innovator who are most easily scapegoated, especially if they are seen to be linked to the enemy in the external world. Such an individual is then selected for attack not only to rid the group of its own death-taintedness, but also in an attempt to promote solidarity by punishing difference. The particular identity of the person chosen for attack is secondary to the social, economic and political context of the attack. Similarly the scapegoats' perceived political identity overrides what may be more personal aspects of their identity. Furthermore, the political identity of the attackers themselves has an unprecedented salience in this context. In fact the attackers frequently engage in what Reicher (1982) termed self-stereotyping. In this process individuals acting in a group define themselves in terms of their group membership (e.g. comrade or security force member) and then conform in rather stereotypical ways to those attributes which they believe define the group (Manganyi, 1990). These may include attributes such as physical prowess and bravery in challenging the *status quo*, attributes which the Leandra group would certainly have identified with as characteristic of a 'comrade'. They would then have acted in terms of these attributes in a group context, and this in a situation of inter-group conflict would certainly have increased the probability of violence (Foster, 1991).

In these terms crowd violence may be seen as a form of social action, the intention of which is to challenge particular power relations (Reicher, 1982). It expresses social, racial, gender and class antagonisms and is a reflection on an ideological understanding by the in-group that out-group members 'are enemies and to that extent can be justifiably attacked' (Manganyi, 1990).

The implication of all these factors in the human burnings which occurred in South Africa is clearly illustrated in the events surrounding a widely publicised case of human burning, namely the killing of Maki Skosana. Two of the Leandra group were in the crowd which witnessed her death, and so its relevance to this study is more than incidental.

Maki Skosana was killed at Duduza (a township some 70 kilometres from Leandra) in July 1985 by a crowd of people who had been attending the funeral of 'comrades' who had died as a result of the premature explosion of some hand-grenades. It was felt that the grenades had been booby-trapped. Skosana was accused of supplying the police with information that allowed them access to these grenades, which were intended for use against the state. These accusations were based on the fact that she had had contact with the deceased comrades just prior to their death. She was also known to have entertained a policeman in her house. There was in fact no hard evidence against Skosana (Soggot, personal comm.). Nevertheless these facts, combined with her image as a non-conformist, made her vulnerable to selection as a scapegoat.

She was very outspoken, and freely criticised members of the community. She had told some of her friends, for example, that they were not committed to the struggle but only attended meetings as social occasions (Soggot, personal comm.). She was also courageous. She had challenged the police on several occasions in the past. These acts, however, did not bring her any praise, even though the objectives she was attempting to achieve would have been popularly supported. Her courageous acts were seen as proof of her complicity with the enemy, as it was argued that she was only able to challenge the police because she was in fact a collaborator (Soggot, personal comm.).

From this is it clear that Skosana was not simply selected randomly as a scapegoat. She was a non-conformist, an independent thinker. She had placed herself outside of the boundary of human sympathy as defined by her particular community through her transgression of a taboo, namely fraternising with a policeman. Her relationship with the putative enemy, in the person of the policeman, defined her as alien and foreign in a context in which few differences could be tolerated. Thus Skosana presented herself as an ideal scapegoat, whether or not there was any validity to the claim that she was an informer. Furthermore, this occurred in a situation which could be defined as atrocity-producing.

The community was in a state of great upheaval, it was under severe threat by an external enemy, namely the state, and its internal structures had been all but destroyed. It had existed for months in a state of great social upheaval in which hierarchies within the group between young and old, teacher and student, parent and child, had been broken down. Numerous traumas had been inflicted on the community in the months preceding the atrocity. The death of the comrades just prior to the burning of Maki Skosana was an especially bitter blow, as they had offered hope that some action against the enemy was possible. It evoked not only feelings of loss, but also of being cheated. Furthermore, events which defied logical explanation, such as indiscriminate arrests, had been visited upon them. Archetypal heroes had arisen to free the community, but they too had been thwarted.

Certainly those who provided descriptions of these events describe their anger at this lost opportunity to hit back, to refuse to submit passively any longer. The readiness of the guerillas who had been killed to risk all stimulated not only great admiration but guilt. People felt guilty that these comrades were prepared to make greater sacrifices than they themselves were. They characterised the deceased as 'ideal comrades' and felt that they fell short of this. In the community at large, feelings of pain, anger and guilt were therefore accumulating prior to the attack on Skosana. The ground was also being laid for an increase in self-stereotyping as the notion of the ideal comrade became more salient.

On the night before she was attacked, there was a night vigil for the comrades. Many people were sleep-deprived, having chanted and danced throughout the night: as a result they were in a state of greatly increased emotional arousal.

By the time of the Duduza atrocity, the group desperately needed to bring under its control the prolonged trauma it had sustained. One means of achieving this was identifying and eliminating what it perceived to be the immediate cause of such trauma. The group needed to turn a passive experience into an active one to engage in radical action which could challenge the *status quo*, to avenge the death of heroes, to exact instant justice, to expiate and purge its own guilt. It needed to give vent to its accumulated rage, pain, humiliation and guilt through the obliteration of a symbol of oppression onto which this could be projected. Skosana provided this symbol. In the eyes of many community members, her guilt was clear. Her life was forfeit, not only to excise threats to the community, but to serve as a warning to others, and to reinforce the notion of the accountability of each individual to the collective. By the time Maki Skosana was attacked, she was already perceived by many to have a dehumanised status.

The attack on her proceeded in stages, beginning with one or two individuals verbally abusing her, pushing her, then hitting her. It gained momentum slowly until it reached a crescendo, at which point Skosana died as a result of the beating she had suffered. Petrol was then poured on her and she was set alight. Even after her death, the crowd continued to abuse her, and a rock was dropped on her head.

Once Skosana had been killed, the need to reaffirm her dehumanised status as a way of justifying the event was intensified. This process of justification manifested itself very clearly in the case studies to be described below. What is also clearly manifested in these case studies is the human diversity of response in relation to such events. These case studies show that even in the moment of crisis, when the group as a whole was in the sway of powerful emotional forces, individuals nevertheless participated and experienced themselves in diverse ways. Some wholly lost their sense of a personal identity, and merged fully with a political identity. Others became dissociated. They split off from themselves and observed themselves in action. Yet others responded with revulsion and repugnance. The following vignettes, gleaned from people who saw themselves as active participants in the events, illustrate these differences. The vignettes are based on reports from the Leandra group as well as from ten youths from other townships on the Witwatersrand who were identified by key informants as having witnessed necklacings or other human burnings.

Stanley

Stanley is good-looking, vibrant and charming. Like Ricky, however, he gives the impression that he needs to assess the interviewer's reactions and to stay constantly attuned to his environment. What made this interview with him so remarkable was the way these qualities disappeared as he spoke of the death of Skosana. His normal style of presentation was totally transformed. He rapidly became oblivious to the interviewer's presence and his general surroundings, as he relived the emotion of the event. He moved from pain when talking of the death of the comrades, through anger, and into excitement as the attack itself was described.

Stanley only showed some awareness of my presence when he described the moment Skosana was set alight. He described in detail the smell of her burning hair, which he said suddenly shocked him into reality. At this point, he reported, he became very fearful. While discussing this episode Stanley grew visibly anxious and tense, as he seemed, in parallel, shocked back into the reality of the interview. He looked directly at me for the first time since the beginning of his narrative. He explained in an embarrassed and anxious way that he had never before experienced a human burning, which was why it had shocked him so deeply in that instant of awareness.

What is striking is that in the interview situation Stanley obviously expected to be condemned for his reaction. It did not occur to him that his participation in the attack itself might be cause for disapprobation, rather than his moment of fear. In anticipating disapproval of his fear rather than his participation in the attack, Stanley was clearly out of touch with my real reactions in the interview. He also perceived me then in a way which was at odds with his normal, expressed perception of me. Stanley normally sees me as far less progressive than himself; in fact, he has communicated to me that he sees me as not radical enough. It was obvious therefore that Stanley's perception of the interview situation was a projection of his own feelings as well as a projection of what he felt the group's response might be. He was clearly responding in terms of self-stereotyping and measuring himself against the notion of the ideal comrade. Furthermore, his demeanour throughout this section of the interview was totally uncharacteristic. He seemed completely absorbed in himself and out of touch with the external situation. This is the antithesis of what is said to occur in the state of deindividuation – a notion frequently invoked to explain individuals' behaviour in groups. In this state the individual is excessively responsive to the external situation.

The state of deindividuation was first described by Festinger, Pepitane and Newcomb in 1952. It is characterised by abandonment of normal self-restraint, loss of individuality and merging of personal consciousness with that of the group. It is facilitated by the anonymity of large groups and by the excitement generated by group activities which focus attention away from the self, reducing self-awareness and self-monitoring and hence self-restraint. In this state of diminished self-awareness, people frequently act without thought and without checking their actions against their own internalised values. Behaviour tends to become disconnected from attitudes and thought, and individuals emulate group behaviour without taking responsibility for their own on an individual level. But the notion of deindividuation has been criticised on the ground that individuals in crowds are not lacking in self-awareness *per se.* They are simply more aware of their social identity and less aware of their personal identity at that moment.

It is clear that this was indeed true for Stanley. But it is also clear from both Stanley's description of his involvement in these events and his demeanour in the interview that he was in a state of greatly heightened emotionality throughout the killing of Skosana, except for the moment her hair was set alight. This event shocked him back into a more personal awareness and also into a more private morality that had not been operating immediately prior to this. In that moment, however, any desire he might have had to distance himself from what was happening was swamped by his fear of the judgment of the group, a fear that was informed by self-stereotyping. Furthermore, the events had also reached a point of no return. To have expressed on a physical level the sudden disjunction between himself and the group in that precise moment was not possible. Instead he he moved back into his political identity, in which he remained to the end of the annihilation of Skosana.

Stanley reports that he suffered symptoms in the aftermath, which would have clearly fitted a diagnosis of post-traumatic stress disorder. He was bothered by intrusive thoughts and recurrent nightmares for weeks. During this time he reconnected once again both with his own individuality and with his own peacetime morality. He reports that he thought continuously about this event, talked about it and prayed about it. What worried him was not that Skosana was killed, for he remained convinced that she was an informer and should have been killed. It was the brutality and cruelty of her death that worried him.

He stressed, however, the symbolic value of her death in strategic terms, in terms of the warning that it sent out to the community. He sees as unfortunate the fact that events such as these brought international disapproval in their wake and were condemned by some black leaders. He nevertheless holds to the belief that the symbolic value of Skosana's death compensated for these negative consequences. Within its particular historical context, he still is convinced that this death was justified.

Stanley believes he was acting as a soldier. He has dedicated his life to the service of the 'will of the people'; at that moment of Skosana's annihilation he perceived it to be clearly expressed and believed he was carrying it out. He does not, in retrospect, construe what happened as an atrocity or an act of gratuitous brutality. He ascribes meaning to it, and so justifies it. In doing so, he affirms his own identity as a freedom fighter prepared to carry out tasks which might go against the grain. He thus imbues his own actions with a morality which transcends ordinary morality, reconstructing it in pro-social rather than anti-social terms.

In imbuing this event with a transcendent morality and a pro-social meaning in terms of the will of the people, Stanley was not acting any differently from others involved in similar events. Kelman (1973), writing in the context of violence against civilians in times of war, discusses this phenomenon in the following terms:

> In certain authority systems, the governing ideology places the highest value on the loyalty of functionaries to the leader as a person or to the organisation. Those committed to such a system may well see it as their duty to follow authoritative orders regardless of their personal preferences. Within their value system the order calls forth what they would consider a moral obligation that overrides any other moral systems they might have. Usual standards of morality are considered inapplicable. Functionaries do not expect to be held personally responsible for their actions. They are agents and extensions of the authorities and thus by definition are assured of their protection.... They identify with the authority system and are caught up in its glory and mystique.

The very act of entering into an authority situation radically changes the perceptions individuals hold of their own actions (Kelman, 1973). The most obvious change is that individuals no longer conceives of themselves as fully responsible for their actions. All initiative can be attributed to those issuing the orders. Furthermore, the individual's evaluation of the self shifts the focus from the morality of the act he or she is performing to how well he or she is doing it.

This description of the intrapsychic functioning of freedom fighters fits very well. For Stanley, the 'authority' in question was not that of a superior officer but that of 'the people'. It is important to bear in mind the rhetoric and rallying cries which prevailed at the time, and still do. The whole basis for mass mobilisation revolves around ideas that 'the people' shall govern. Slogans continually refer to 'the power of the people'. The notion of the collective as the ultimate authority was, and to some extent remains, the dominant ideology in the townships. The importance of individual accountability to the group, to the community and to the people is constantly stressed.

In this context, the idea that the group could have an authoritative hold over individuals, similar to that of a superior officer, becomes feasible. This authority would be further compounded by all the normal horizontal peer-group pressures to which adolescents are subject. Thus, in this situation, the pressure exerted by the group and by the 'will of the people' on those who feel morally bound to respond to these pressures would be enormous.

In evaluating Stanley's description of these events, it is important to bear in mind that it is a reconstruction after the event, following months of concerted effort on his part to come to terms with it. In this sense it reflects his final psychic resolution of what happened, rather than an accurate reconstruction of what actually occurred for him at the time.

The clinical impression formed during his interview was that much of the personal agency and transcendent morality to which he retrospectively lays claim is exaggerated. His whole demeanour while relaying the event was almost trance-like. He was clearly in the sway of strong emotions, even in its recall. The raw anger and excitement that he had clearly experienced re-emerged in the room. These emotions, even in recall, were extraordinarily powerful. In their original expression, they would surely have undermined Stanley's capacity for self-regulation.

Even in the moment of being shocked by the horror of the event, his decision to continue to participate was informed by his fear that the group might turn on him if it sensed his withdrawal. This fear was itself informed by the authority relationship he had assumed. It was also informed by his sense of how the ideal comrade would behave and the salience this aspect of his identity had in that moment. Despite this, Stanley experienced himself as having a choice, and it was this subjective area of choice which provided him with a lifeline in his subsequent integration of the event into his identity. The sense that he had a choice made Stanley feel that his behaviour was under his own control, and that the event made sense in an overall pattern within his primary idéntity as a freedom fighter.

On a theoretical level, Stanley's description of these events lends some support to the idea that during war the ego splits and organises itself in terms of two moralities, one pertaining to war and one pertaining to peace. In the theoretical literature it is generally assumed that these moralities are then maintained very separately from one another and that any collision of one with the other will provoke a psychological breakdown. However, in Stanley's case, it would appear that some interpenetration of the two realities is possible without breakdown, provided that both realities can be encompassed by some overriding moral principle and integrated into an ego which can accommodate both. It is clear that Stanley is not currently presenting with clinical anxiety, depression, post-traumatic stress disorder or psychosomatic symptomatology of an order sufficient to disrupt his everyday functioning. Nor is he indulging in indiscriminate anti-social and violent behaviour in his everyday life.

In reviewing Stanley's involvement in the killing of Skosana, one of the most interesting features that emerges is the degree to which he felt that he had actually participated in the killing. In reality he was not one of the persons directly responsible for Skosana's death. In view of this, and the condemnation expressed by leaders he admired of this killing, and given his own qualms about its cruelty, it is surprising that he did not distance himself from it; in other words, it is surprising that he did not capitalise on his non-involvement in the killing rather than emphasising his involvement.

However, this option, had he chosen it, would have required that he question why he had not intervened to prevent the killing of Skosana in the first place. It would also have put his own courage and morality into question; and he would have had to question his sanity and the sanity of the group at the time. The consequent degree of reordering of his inner world would have been overwhelming.

Whatever his difficulties in integrating his identity as a 'freedom fighter', one thing Stanley did not do was to pervert the metaphor and give himself permission to express a well of repressed anger and take personal revenge in its name. In this he differed from a number of his peers, for example Mdani, whose case vignette follows.

Mdani

Mdani is thin and wiry. His hair is closely cropped and he is poorly dressed. He has a certain waif-like quality. In the interview situation he was withdrawn and morose. It was clear that Mdani had certain misgivings about the interview, and that while he had agreed to participate as a favour to one of the key informants, he experienced the research situation as an intrusion and was deeply distrustful of it.

He was particularly reluctant to speak of his home life which, it seems, was generally unhappy. He was similarly reluctant to speak of his current life and involvement in the struggle. He only became slightly animated when he mentioned Maki Skosana. His disparagement of and contempt for her seemed to bring him to life. He stressed how treacherous, promiscuous and destructive she was. He felt at the time – and still feels – that she deserved everything that had happened to her.

Mdani, like Stanley, did not in any way participate directly in the killing. He observed her death from some physical distance, as part of the crowd. However, like Stanley, he identified with the group mood, and felt at one with the anger and hatred directed toward Skosana. He did not describe the events at Duduza in any detail, and all questioning failed to elicit further information. Instead, he focused on his personal feelings toward Skosana.

Unlike Stanley, Mdani did not stress the strategic value of this event. He did not place it in a broader context within the struggle. He focused instead on Skosana's personal qualities. He seemed to use the situation as some outlet for his own angry and destructive impulses. Any cathartic relief he might have achieved through this expression of rage and anger seems, however, to have been temporary. He certainly does not seem to have been purged and healed through this. If anything, his participation in this act reinforces his need for a cathartic expression of emotion through violence, and in his private life he is in fact highly volatile and aggressive. In general terms, he tends to have a disinhibited relationship with aggression. He is frequently involved in alcohol- and drug-related fights, as an individual and as part of a group.

His aggression seems to be self-reinforcing: Mdani reports that he often feels better after a fight. Apparently, expressing aggression reduces tension, and this relatively pleasant feeling acts as its own reward. The acting out of aggression in Mdani's case weakens inhibition against the expression of further aggression and this gradually allows for the expression of increasing levels of violence. This dynamic, whereby a relatively mild expression of aggression which is unchecked then acts to disinhibit more violent expressions of aggression, certainly operated in the crowd at Duduza, in that the attack on Maki Skosana began in fairly restrained fashion as she was pushed and jostled by a section of the crowd; as these acts were not met with sufficient resistance, they escalated in intensity and culminated in her death.

In Mdani, Darwin's axiom that 'he who gives way to violent gestures will increase his rage' (quoted in Myers, 1988, p. 436) seems to be realised. There is little indication that he experiences either guilt or remorse in relation to his aggressive outbursts. He is habituated to aggression and, at the time of the interview, seemed effectively numbed to it. Unlike Stanley, Mdani showed few signs of compassion or remorse. He does not report having been unduly concerned about the episode and he indicates that it did not preoccupy him or worry him afterwards.

Mdani's violent actions were not integrated into a deeply felt identification with an ideal of comradeship or the value of the liberation struggle nor did they form part of a deeply felt transcendent morality. His justifications for his own actions were superficial. The victims were simply presented as deserving of their fate. His conscience did not require the same elaborate and sophisticated system of defence that Stanley's did. His actions seemed to be informed by what would bring immediate relief of his own psychic pain. He appears to anaesthetise himself through alcohol and drugs and to act out his pain rather than feel his way through it. Psychic pain has been disowned and split off, as have humiliated and despised parts of the self.

Unlike Stanley, Mdani is chronically anti-social. His participation in the struggle seems incidental both to the killing of Skosana and to many other aspects of his life. The struggle at times provides him with a socially sanctioned outlet for his aggression, and this partially motivates his participation in it. However, in the absence of this outlet he actively seeks out others.

Exposure to violence has damaged Mdani. His experiences in the intimacy of the home and in school where he was subjected to harsh corporal punishment, as well as exposure to the generally violent conditions in the township, have all laid the groundwork of damage upon which political violence has been superimposed. Mdani's exposure to political violence as a victim has increased his feelings of helplessness and rage, exacerbated his trauma and increased his desire for revenge. Acting upon this desire has further damaged him, as it has eroded his conscience and further impaired his capacity for concern. Unlike Stanley, who is violent only when in fairly extreme circumstances, Mdani is violent under conditions of far less extremity. More important, he actively seeks out those circumstances which enhance the disinhibition of the deeply felt, tension-inducing rage he carries within him.

In his active seeking of circumstances which will allow the free expression of violence, he is the antithesis of Claire, who will seek to avoid all such circumstances. Mdani experiences very little subjective psychic distress following his own violent actions because he has not internalised strong superego inhibitions against them, and he has little empathy for vulnerability in himself or in the other. In this sense Mdani is the epitome of the 'brutalised youth' depicted in the media in the 1984–1986 period. However, it is clear that while Mdani does indeed conform to the image, he is not representative of black youth. In fact, in conforming to the image of 'brutalised youth' Mdani highlights by contrast those who do not conform, including Claire, whose capacity for empathy is intact and who experienced a great deal of psychic distress because of her exposure to events which offended her sensibility and cut across a well-defined and refined superego.

Claire

Claire is large and matronly, despite her relative youth. There is a strange combination of strength and vulnerability in her presentation. There is also something very self-contained and centred about her.

Claire was present at the assault and attempted murder of a policeman in Soweto. He too was doused with petrol and set alight, but unlike Skosana, managed to escape. The event occurred under similar circumstances, in a period of particularly intense repression in the townships, with a higher-than-usual number of deaths, detentions and injuries. It followed a public meeting when feelings in the group were running at fever pitch, and the policeman became an ideal scapegoat. Like Skosana, he was assaulted, beaten, intimidated and harassed before the attempt on his life was made.

Claire was a witness to the entire procedure. From the outset, she experienced herself as separate from the group who attacked the policeman. She did not identify with the group and felt overwhelmed by its anger and hatred. However, during the assault, she felt rooted to the spot, totally unable to free herself from the emotional grip of the situation or unable physically to remove herself. She felt bound to what was happening by some intangible, magnetic power. She felt repelled, but at the same time transfixed, almost hypnotised by horror. Waves of nausea swept over her. Yet she could not remove herself. She described a sense of compulsion to remain and observe, like a snake before a mongoose.

Claire was haunted by this experience for months. Even as she spoke of it in the interview, her voice was tremulous, and it was clearly still an unresolved episode in her life. For months she could not sleep, she had nightmares, and during the day she was plagued by intrusive thoughts. She had difficulty eating, especially meat. She still cannot stomach the smell of frying meat as it reminds her too vividly of what happened.

Claire has spent a great deal of time and psychic energy attempting to come to terms with it. She still berates herself for not attempting to intervene to prevent the attack; as far as she is concerned, it throws her integrity into question. She regrets that she did not leave the group sooner, and that she participated in the singing, dancing and chanting that preceded the attack. She links the emotional build-up in the group with the subsequent attack, and profoundly regrets her involvement in this build-up, even though she could not have guessed what would happen.

In reflecting upon her experience, Claire feels that she has been violated in some way by it. The core of her humanness has been contaminated and infected. Claire's depiction of her psychic state mirrors that of the soldiers studied by Lifton (1973) who had internalised what he calls a death imprint. Lifton describes memories of deaths inflicted or witnessed that evoke feelings of guilt about the transgression of that which should have remained sacrosanct. These feelings of guilt in turn activate the death imprint or memory traces, and a pernicious circuit is established from which escape is almost impossible.

Claire explains her experience in spiritual terms, in terms of good and evil. She felt a powerful spirit grip the group and take possession of it. She is not sure why she escaped its possession or how she managed to remain in some way apart. However, she blames this spirit for the 'evil' that erupted.

Claire's relationship to what happened in Soweto and to the issue of violence in general is, however, ambivalent. While on an emotional level her whole being revolted against the attack she witnessed, she does not eschew the use of violence in the struggle. On an intellectual level, she embraces the notion of a just war, and believes that it is justifiable to kill the enemy. Her arguments against violence revolve more around the difficulties involved in identifying the enemy clearly than in a condemnation of violence itself. Claire believes that in the South African situation, the establishment of innocence or guilt with absolute certainty is almost impossible, citing in support of her argument known instances of policemen and Defence Force members who have turned out to be members of the ANC.

It was apparent on interviewing Claire that her views were informed by her gut-level aversive response to inflicting pain and taking human life. It was also clear, however, that she was constrained from simply going along with this gut-level reaction. Some of her friends were implicated in the violence; moreover, freedom has not yet been won. This places her in a situation of conflict between her emotional responses to brutality, her ability to see this brutality in a broader perspective, and her loyalty to friends who might have been implicated.

She lives uneasily with this tension. She remains in touch with the complexity of her emotions and with the ambiguities in her world, at great psychic cost. She lives with far greater levels of consciously felt anxiety and depression than do Mdani or even Stanley. She also complains of headaches and stomach pains and numerous other psychosomatic ailments. She has not repressed the memories of the violence which she witnessed, but has neither learned to live with them. They cut profoundly across her sense of self and her worldview. They mark the end of innocence, even in a world which has been frequently punctuated by cruel events.

Benedict

Benedict was present at the same burning of the policeman in Soweto. He is less articulate than Claire, and was far more reluctant to discuss either the event or his reactions to it. During the interview, he showed little emotion and seemed to be quite cut off from the experience. Far more than Claire, he mouths the common justifications of attacks on symbols of the state. He seems, however, to cling to these justifications without any real conviction. They allow him to rationalise his behaviour in particular situations, but they are not part of a broader system of meaning for him as they are for Stanley. They are used more to justify the raw expression of emotion.

Benedict speaks with feeling of the hardship visited upon the community by the police in general. His dislike, fear and anger in this regard are obvious. When he speaks of the particular policeman who was attacked in Soweto, however, his feelings are more in conflict. Unlike the people of Soweto involved in the attack, he had no personal knowledge of the victim: his exposure to the events was not invested with the immediacy and intensity that others may have felt.

He feels strongly that all policemen need to be educated on a political level and to be held accountable to the community. Failing this, they need to be disciplined and punished. However, he himself did not need to punish the particular policeman who was attacked, and in fact was alienated from the group as a result of their attack. He felt that the discipline meted out to this policeman was too severe. He was unable to verbalise this to the group at the time of the event and afterwards. The event had a momentum of its own in which it was almost impossible to intervene without putting himself in danger. Afterwards, however, his overriding feeling was one of isolation. He believed that the group had been wrong, and this cut him off from them. He felt that he was the one out of step, that he alone had views on the subject that differed. He imagined that they had a consensus from which he was excluded.

Benedict reports that during the crisis he experienced himself subjectively as a spectator, not only of the event, but of himself. He did not use these words, but spoke of his spirit leaving his body, which continued to act in the absence of his spirit. His spirit, however, did not leave the site. It remained there but did not 're-enter my body until the policeman had run away'.

His description of this experience seems to fit the well-known phenomenon of depersonalisation. One of the primary characteristics of this state is that individuals experience themselves as outside of the body, as if the spirit has indeed left the body. Accompanying this is a sense of detachment, a subjective sense that events are not happening to the self but to a stranger, and that it is a stranger and not the self which is acting.

The subjective sense of a separation between the observing and participating self is so overwhelming in these states that many individuals with no prior religious beliefs have subsequently become convinced of the separate existence of the soul. The mystical dimension with which this experience is invested is strengthened by the fact that depersonalisation frequently occurs in life-threatening situations. In fact, in the psychological literature depersonalisation is characterised as an adaptive response to such predicaments.

Fear of death is one of the most profound and basic fears. When it is stimulated, its potential to overwhelm the organism and interfere with appropriate responses is clearly very great. The split between the observing and participating self is a way of facilitating both hyper-alertness with regard to the external world, and dampening of stimulation in the internal world. This is vital in an extreme situation in which the organism needs to establish some control over incoming stimulation while at the same time preparing to act. This delicate balancing act produces a number of perceptual side-effects. As the individual's attention is increasingly focused on the extremity of demand in the present, the past and future recede. The individual becomes divorced from the continuity of events. Normal consciousness, 'which is like a film strip of frames which merge with one another', becomes frozen and may lose its location in time and space (Noyes & Kletti, 1976).

The sense of timelessness which is created by this, and the split into an observing and participating self which occurs, all lend themselves to mystical interpretations such as those given by Benedict, namely that his spirit left his body. It is true that Benedict's own life was not threatened in the context in which the depersonalisation occurred. However, the crowd was extremely volatile, and the potential of such crowds to turn their wrath against the non-conformist was recognised by all individuals interviewed. In addition, the acts in which the crowd was engaged were intrinsically of an order that would threaten psychic integration and wholeness.

The defence of depersonalisation gave Benedict the maximum opportunity to retain psychic integration both during and after the event. At the time it allowed him to continue to act and perform as if he were part of the crowd, an adaptive function in terms of physical survival. Simultaneously, his sense that he was not inhabiting his body allowed him to be distant from an experience he found unacceptable. This separation also allowed him to distance himself in retrospect. He could exonerate himself from the responsibility of participation. From a psychic perspective, he could take refuge in the notion that no matter what his actions had been, they were not really animated by his own spirit; it was not he who had participated.

Schilder (1953), one of the foremost researchers on the experience of depersonalisation, proposed that depersonalisation serves as a defence against experience itself. By increasing their self-observation, depersonalised individuals negate the actual experience of the moment. In life-threatening situations, this serves to protect the individual from the pain that would be generated by confronting death.

It is not surprising therefore that in the interview with Benedict he did not seem unduly distressed, as Claire was, by what he had witnessed. He also did not seem to have struggled with issues after the event as Stanley did. In one way or another he sealed it off into a closed compartment of his mind. He indicated that it only intruded upon him for a few days after it had happened. Furthermore, what he found most disturbing about this intrusion was not the image of the policeman in distress, but the feelings of alienation from the group that their actions evoked in him.

Benedict, like most adolescents, is still in the process of consolidating his identity. His sense of well-being is highly dependent upon a sense of continuity between his self-defined identity and values, and those of his reference group. Breaks of such magnitude in this continuity challenge not only the value system of individuals, but their identities. He clearly lacked the resources to integrate what happened and to evaluate it in his own terms. He sought instead to re-establish as quickly as possible a sense of continuity with his peers and their values, to protect his well-being and identity.

He was aided in this endeavour by the fact that the attack had not taken place on his home territory. By leaving Soweto, which he did one week later, he was able to encapsulate this discontinuity. It helped him isolate this experience psychologically while he reconnected with his peers in Leandra.

Benedict reports that on his return to Leandra, he did not talk a great deal about what had transpired in Soweto. However, those people with whom he did discuss the matter agreed with him that the punishment the Soweto group had exacted was excessive. They confirmed him in his original perception and in so doing re-established for him a connectedness between himself and his reference group. This priority superseded more internal, intrapsychic concerns about the morality of what transpired in Soweto and his part in it.

In reflecting upon events as gruesome as human burnings, it is impossible to refrain from value judgments. Nor is it desirable to do so. Atrocities are clearly always to be condemned, and individuals must be held responsible for their actions. However, the assessment of moral blameworthiness on a personal level is extraordinarily complex. As has been revealed in the case studies, simple observation of the behaviour of an individual engaged in crowd violence reveals little about the state of mind, motivation, or the degree to which the individual shares a 'common purpose' with the violence of the crowd. Given the number of prosecutions of individuals for murder and assault which occurred in South Africa under the aegis of 'common purpose', this is an important point to note.

When violence can be justified within individuals' own existing system of morality, it creates few psychological problems for them at least in the medium term. However, while the exercise of violence seems to create few problems for the individual on a personal level, it would also seem that it does not solve many problems either. In the Leandra study, for example, there was no evidence that participation in violence had a healing or transforming effect at the individual level. In the immediate aftermath of public violence, there may well have been a short-lived euphoria but this was seldom sustained. That violence served a group function, that it bound individuals together and that it might have contributed to bringing about structural changes of ultimate benefit to the individual, is not disputed. However, in this study at least, violence as such did not transform individuals or cure their psychological wounds, even though it might have facilitated a sense of empowerment and well-being in the short term. There was indeed evidence that violence may have been used by certain individuals as a way of reducing tension and also as a way of avoiding depression or anxiety in the short term, as in the case of Mdani. However, when used in this way, it seems to have had an addictive rather than a curative effect. The violence generated bore an intensity of emotion which was then sought in its own right.

Crises of the order described above usually act to mobilise strategies of adaptation that have proved their worth, and the strategies discussed in this chapter have proved effective for the youth in varying degrees. This does not mean, however, that they adapted to the events of 1984–86 easily or that their own behaviour, especially their own violent behaviour, was integrated into their sense of self without struggle. When atrocities were involved, most reported that they initially had been traumatised and that they had felt some guilt, even though this may not have been sustained.

The capacity of most members of the group to feel guilt was the most optimistic finding of this study when contemplating the re-integration of youth into ordinary civilian life in the future. Guilt is an essential component in community living. The ability to induce guilt in members of society is vital to the survival of modern societies which cannot monitor behaviour directly all the time. It is the induction of guilt that ensures the conformity which makes collective living possible. While an excess of guilt may create distress for individuals on a personal level, the absence of the capacity to feel guilt, if it were to characterise large groups of people, would spell disaster for community living. Both the alleviation of guilt, and a proper appreciation of its significance, are crucial when considering the reintegration of individuals and communities traumatised by war. Certainly in the new South Africa, where education for peace will have to be a priority, such issues will have to be considered. The final chapter of this book concerns itself with the issue of education for peace.

6   Towards the Future

As South Africa enters the 1990s, despite talks about negotiations, civil strife continues. In fact, the opening years of the decade have proved to be as bloody as any in South Africa's history. The current ubiquitousness and intensity of violence has sustained media attention on the question of whether violence has become endemic in black townships. Discussions with a number of the Leandra youths about their own views on the current violence revealed a diversity of opinion. Many agreed that they as the youth were very militant as a group, but not that they were out of control. They felt rather that their contribution at the forefront of the struggle was being undervalued, that they were not sufficiently recognised as partners in the negotiating process. They were concerned about the degree of representation they would finally be afforded in negotiations, and the extent to which issues directly affecting them would be on the agenda. There was a feeling that they had forfeited many of the privileges of childhood to participate in the struggle. They could not now be expected simply to go back to accepting old hierarchies, whether in the family, the school or the broader political arena. They felt that they had entered adulthood prematurely to take on the mantle of the freedom fighter, which had irrevocably changed their perception of themselves and their place in society. This did not mean that they did not respect older people, but this respect had to be mutual and had to be earned. The very notion that they needed to be brought under control evoked anger in many of those interviewed. 'We have fought for freedom, we have no education, no jobs and we are too old for school. These problems need to be solved. This is the problem, not the violence.'

Others agreed that discipline was a major problem and felt that community organisations needed to be strengthened to keep individuals under control. They acknowledged, however, that it was perhaps in the nature of youth to act rather than to deliberate, and pointed to the efficacy of action over debate in the 1970s and 1980s.

It is precisely this tendency of youth to act which is being criticised at the present time by those who feel it is disrupting constructive peace initiatives. There are, however, others who believe that these peace initiatives are premature and constitute a sell-out. This sector of the community has a more positive view of the continued militancy of youth, as do those who believe that armed self-protection against vigilante violence is the only option open to them.

Whatever value one places on civil strife, the real concerns of this project remain the effects of violence on the individual psyche. Even when exposure to civil strife does not lead to breakdown, it still changes the individual's consciousness in fundamental ways. It encourages categorical thinking and sharp divisions between those considered to be friends and those thought of as foes. The dangers of this kind of thinking were quite apparent at Wilgespruit. It became clear how easily individuals who were generally sympathetic to the group could come to be regarded as enemies because of disagreements over relatively minor issues. In regard to certain staff members, for example, large areas of agreement were overlooked, and alliances which could have been formed were in fact undermined.

This process was aggravated by the Leandra group's inflexibility in their approach to problem-solving. They used the same coercive tactics in bargaining with friends as they used with enemies. There was thus an over-generalisation of the contexts in which it might have been appropriate to be coercive rather than persuasive.

However, the exercise of violence by the Leandra group remained relatively context-specific, under the control of moral principles which could be articulated. This was true despite their tendency to over-generalise the situations in which it was appropriate to express aggression, and then to justify this intellectually. There was no evidence that the majority of youth had become amoral or insensitive to the broader social context in which they lived. On the contrary, they showed themselves to be imbued with a great deal of pro-social sentiment as expressed in the metaphor of the 'freedom fighter', whose brief extends beyond that of the 'warrior-hero'. In a peacetime society, this metaphor will be crucial in helping individuals realign their identities.

In addition to affecting their psychological development, the engagement of young people in civil strife has also acted in purely practical ways to limit their opportunities to learn skills more appropriate to peacetime life. It has further limited their already grossly inadequate access to schooling and to occupational career paths. In addition, it has shown them that authorities, including parental authorities, can be challenged, disobeyed and even coerced, with relative impunity.

In probing what the Leandra group saw as the difficulties in reestablishing a social order geared to peace, with particular regard to the issue of adult authority, one found a distinction in their thinking about the relationship between parents and children in the political arena, as opposed to the field of social relationships. Differences in opinion between parents and children were seen to be sharpest in the political sphere. Respect for parents in the area of social and family matters was strongly supported, and it was only in the political arena that it was felt that parents should be consistently challenged. Even in political matters, it was pointed out youth organisations saw themselves as accountable to civic associations, and to progressive parent associations. They acknowledged that proper consultation did not always occur in practice; nevertheless, the philosophy underpinning youth organisations stressed this accountability to other authorities. The youth at Wilgespruit clearly desired both acceptance and guidance from older people. There was, in fact, an idealisation of symbolic parental figures, including local community leaders and well-known political figures. Many of the youth presented as heroes not only in search of a script, but also in search of a credible script-writer.

This bodes well for the future, for it implies that if credible leaders put energy into writing credible scripts for a peacetime scenario, youth will live into them, provided, of course, that some of their real grievances are alleviated and their legitimate aspirations met. The material conditions in which these youth find themselves will remain the central factor dictating their behaviour and attitudes. If these conditions are not improved they will continue to react negatively, using the forms of protest with which they are most familiar. Similarly, if an alliance between vigilantes and the police is perceived to continue, then expectations that youth refrain from violence will inevitably be disappointed.

South Africa has not yet adequately made the structural changes necessary for peace. However, if these changes are brought about, the psychological stance of the majority of youth interviewed in this study is such that, at present, accommodation to a peaceful society is entirely possible. While there are casualties and individuals who have become chronically anti-social, these are still the minority. There was little evidence in the majority of unwillingness to expand their self-concepts beyond the narrowly defined warrior-hero.

The findings of this study that youth are still able to adapt to peace despite exposure to war confirm those obtained by researchers in other contexts. Reynolds (1989), who studied children and youth involved in the war in Zimbabwe, commented on the seeming ease with which a realignment of power within families, schools and communities took place after liberation. After the war, families and communities were able to re-establish hierarchies and to bring children and youth under the control of adults.

One of the factors which Reynolds believes facilitated the re-establishment of control was the care that was taken to acknowledge the role of youth in the war and to recognise the impact of this upon them. She emphasised the importance in the rural areas particularly of formal rituals, conducted by traditional healers, of purification and forgiveness for those who had participated in violence, and showed how such rituals facilitated their absorption back into the community. The rituals invariably involved the elements of confession and acts of reparation by the perpetrator, and absolution by the injured party. Furthermore, these rituals focused not only on the individual, but also on the relationship between the individual and the community, in recognition of the fact that the disturbances of war occur primarily at the interface of individual and community.

The psychological functions of purification rituals have not only been recognised by traditional healers in Africa. In certain North American Indian societies, for example, there are prescribed rituals for handling many common reactions to war. The psychic numbing which accompanies exposure to war is explicitly dealt with in these rituals and in the taboos which have to be observed by returning warriors. They are isolated from everybody except older warriors, and are explicitly forbidden to touch or feed themselves, or to have sexual intercourse, in recognition of the difficulties around intimacy which exposure to violence creates. Their internal numbing is thus externalised and given a shared social meaning (Mansfield, 1982).

Purification ceremonies which follow this isolation serve to cleanse warriors of the toxifying effects of exposure to killing. It is recognised that not only is war polluting, but that the emotional intensity it generates can also be addictive, that warriors will never be the people they were before. It is also understood that new roles have to be created for them, designed to give them special responsibility for educating and caring for others, and drawing on the spiritual wisdom that they are now thought to have acquired. The entry of returning warriors into these new roles is preceded by ceremonies of death and rebirth which symbolically acknowledge their struggle to forge a new pro-social identity.

The intuitive understanding embodied in these rituals of the trauma which war creates is profound. As Silver and Wilson (1988) point out, they do not simply reframe a negative experience. They explicitly utilise strengths gained through being a survivor and by emphasising pro-social attributes, allow for a balancing of the anti-social acts that are committed in war.

It is not only traditional healers but all ministers of religion who are ideally placed to deal with disturbances at this interface. Given the large number of people in South Africa traumatised by war who may belong to one or another church, the services of these individuals will be crucial in facilitating the reintegration process.

The church, given its understanding of the notions of evil, justice and reconciliation, has an established framework from within which to deal with these issues. This is true not only in regard to rituals of purification and forgiveness for the perpetrators of violence, but also in regard to issues pertaining to justice and reconciliation, as they affect victims of violence.

We ignore at our peril the Old Testament law of an eye for an eye and a tooth for a tooth. The revenge motif is found throughout human history, for good reason. It reflects basic human reactions and desires. In speaking of reconciliation therefore, it would be naive to ignore human desires for retribution. It is not easy for people to embrace the notion of reconciliation at the best of times, and it is almost impossible to do so if there is not some sense that justice has been done. The challenge for the church and for those working on issues of reconciliation will be to redirect the desire for revenge and punitive action into constructive ways of achieving justice. Intensive workshops which encourage a linking of justice with reparation by the oppressors rather than retribution against them will be helpful in this regard. Such a link is certainly compatible with Christian doctrine and with many traditional African beliefs.

The importance of mobilising resources within the community itself to facilitate reintegration and to heal its own wounds cannot be overemphasised. Attempts to deal through central control with problems like the disinhibition of aggression among youth will be doomed to failure. Countries which have attempted this by setting up, for example, development brigades have had little success.

Local communities in South Africa have already shown themselves to be remarkably resourceful in generating solutions to their own problems. A case in point would be the people's courts and disciplinary committees established in 1984–86. Despite the excesses of these courts, it has to be acknowledged that they were initially successful in controlling criminal activities, as were the anti-crime campaigns conducted during this period. It is true that these campaigns broke down later as leaders were arrested and less experienced and less disciplined persons took on these tasks. Nevertheless, their initial success points to the problem-solving resources available at community level.

The recognition of the community as one of the appropriate levels of social organisation to mobilise in problem resolution makes sense not only on a political and pragmatic level, but also at the level of individual healing. The crises that wars provoke are primarily at the interface of the individual and the community. The engagement of the community in the healing process is therefore crucial.

Alternative strategies aimed at reintegrating youth into a peaceful society may involve strengthening parental control within families by encouraging the men, some of whom it would appear have opted out of family life, once again to take a more active part in family affairs. Organisations such as trade unions could be consulted and involved in this endeavour. Where large numbers in a community are employed in any one particular industry, the help of the trade union concerned with this industry could be sought. The union could be approached and asked to promote not only civic responsibility, but also to run programmes aimed at family responsibility among its membership. Such an approach would clearly be more viable in some areas than others. In the rural areas where large numbers of men are migrant labourers and women have evolved means of coping with their absence, attempts to reinvolve the men might be more complicated. The need then to generate and support local solutions to local problems is clear, particularly in a situation characterised by the diversity that pertains in South Africa where there are rural–urban divides, divides between large urban townships and peri-urban areas, and many other divisions. The allocation of resources needs, however, to be centrally controlled so that they are equitably distributed.

In the short term, in looking to reintegrate individuals into the community it might be of benefit to draw on lessons learnt in the context of the relationship between groups of displaced persons and sanctuary centres. This set of problems will hopefully dissipate after the cessation of the civil conflict, but at present it remains an area of concern for large numbers of people. One of the most important lessons which the Wilgespruit experience taught us was the importance of managing the relationship between the group and the sanctuary centre which receives it. It is vital that a great deal of time be spent on working out mutual expectations if the group is to stay at the centre for any length of time. The group should be actively engaged in its own maintenance. The election of committees to represent the group and to deal with crises around issues such as health, education and recreation must be facilitated at the outset. In addition, in consultation with the displaced people, a structured programme for the day's activities must be negotiated. The time period for which the group can anticipate being sheltered must be clearly spelt out.

The development of any dependence by the group on the centre should be avoided, as it encourages regression and the dissolution of other defences. Therapeutic approaches in this situation should not promote regression, either in individuals or in the group. They should be geared to helping the members analyse their predicament and formulate strategies for their return to their own communities as soon as possible. In other words, therapeutic approaches should be geared to facilitating and maintaining the individual's functioning in the world.

When this has been impaired by the level of trauma sustained, the provision of didactic input on the common effects of trauma can be useful. Normalising the symptoms and mobilising peer support rather than attempting catharsis is the treatment of choice in contexts such as sanctuary centres, where dependence and regression are to be avoided.

Healing rituals which occur spontaneously in the group, including chanting, dancing and singing, provide natural outlets for emotion in a contained way and should be used wherever possible. Interventions which are more individualised and geared toward catharsis are, however, sometimes necessary when it is clear that there are levels of disturbance which cannot be contained either by didactic effort or by the healing potential of the group itself.

The need for healing practices which respect traditional beliefs was very clear at Wilgespruit and once again highlighted the important role that traditional healers and church leaders can play in the aftermath of war. The knowledge of Western professionals with regard to post-traumatic stress, the group dynamics of displaced persons, and so on, may be helpful to these healers, and should therefore be made available to them if they want it. However, Western professionals should also attempt to understand traditional explanations and solutions in regard to psychological distress if they are to attempt to alleviate it in individuals who retain traditional beliefs (Gumede, 1990).

A great amount of repair work will be needed in the future. The services of all who are capable of acting therapeutically will therefore be required. Help will be required in terms of rehabilitation and prevention of further damage for both black and white youth. The relationship of white youth to violence has not been explored in this book, but there is no doubt that the psyches of white youth, like those of their black counterparts, have been affected by the context of civil strife in which they live. The violent context of news reports, the security gates in their homes, the bomb drills at school, the militarisation of cadets, and for those in the army the violence active duty has brought will all take their toll as will the notions of racial superiority and racial hatred on which many have been reared.

The violence to which white youth have been exposed, and in which they have participated, may have been more subtle, involving prejudice, petty cruelty in the home toward domestic workers, and indifference to the humanity of blacks in general, but it will require no less attention and redress in the future. In fact the subtle, less obvious nature of this violence as well as its pervasiveness might make its effects even more difficult to remedy. It is well known that what is most detrimental to the development of youth is not particular incidents of trauma but the existence of enduring conditions which distort their ability to develop their true potential.

Civil strife is an example of one such social condition, and certainly in this study civil strife was shown to be ultimately detrimental to many of those exposed to it despite the lack of a demonstrable one-to-one relationship between level of exposure to civil strife and incidence of breakdown. The effects of civil strife are inextricably linked with the social conditions that generate it but this does not make its effects less pernicious.

The final conclusion of this book is therefore that exposure to civil strife is emotionally hurtful to youth. The apparent resilience of many youth in the face of civil strife is a tribute to the human spirit's capacity to deal with adversity. It does not invalidate the fact that such strife exposes the young to trauma such as injury, death, homelessness and the loss of loved ones. These traumas will undoubtedly break the spirits of many and will force others into the development of adaptational patterns which may facilitate their survival in the short term but which will limit their development in the long term.

These limitations may be overcome in time and some individuals in the long term may even be strengthened by their experiences of hardship, but taken overall the losses inflicted on youth by civil strife will always outweigh the gains. In evaluating resilience and survival the role of luck and chance should not be underestimated. Nor should those who don't survive be blamed or thought of as weak. Every person has his or her breaking point and those who survive civil strife are those lucky enough not to have been taxed to this point (Garmezy, 1990). Even for those who survive, loss of innocence and early exposure to violence and cruelty have their price. Civil strife by itself may not be as damaging to the individual as the poverty and inequality which generate it but it certainly compounds the effects of all adversity. Furthermore, it adds a dimension to the suffering these conditions engender and this suffering is not erased by the power and dignity which resistance might confer upon those who participate in it.

Even more important than therapeutic intervention will be the implementation of social policies aimed not only at eradicating the root causes of civil strife but at deliberately and self-consciously facilitating the development of the young. We know what facilitates the psychological development of youth and protects them most effectively from breakdown – the establishment of strong, enduring emotional bonds with consistent caretakers. All social policies in the future will therefore need to be evaluated deliberately and self-consciously to assess their impact on the capacity of caretakers to provide adequate child care both at home and in the workplace (Richter, 1990). The needs of children and families must be a priority in any society, but where discriminatory social policies have been enshrined in laws actively undermining black family life, this takes on a particular urgency. Families remain at this point the most accessible and the most successful units for providing child care and they should thus be supported in all their diverse forms. For in the final analysis, it will be the degree to which proper nurturance and care for all South African children is provided, and the degree to which they are socialised toward tolerance, that will determine the extent to which South African youth can be transformed from faces in a revolution to whole persons in a peaceful world.

Appendix: Methodology

This study was based on in-depth interviews with a group of Leandra activists, both at the time of their sojourn at Wilgespruit and again three years later. At Wilgespruit the group comprised 60 individuals (19 girls and 41 boys) ranging in age from 12 to 22 years; the median age was 16. They thus fell into the Western category of middle adolescence. This category, however, is not used by township dwellers themselves, who prefer the term 'youth', which spans the period from about 10 to 30 years. This term has therefore generally been used.

I originally went to Wilgespruit as a counsellor, to offer a service. Research was not on the agenda. Thus material collected at this point was not obtained in any systematic fashion. However, clinical case histories were recorded at the time and were available for approximately one-third of the group. These case histories included background information about family circumstances, schooling, the processes whereby the individual had been inducted into the struggle, attitudes to violence, and individual responses to various traumas.

In addition to these case histories, the clinical impressions of eight of the ten counsellors were obtained in in-depth interviews approximately three months after the experience. The author also participated in monthly peer-group meetings with the counsellors over a two-year period, during which case studies were presented and discussions took place on common problems encountered in the treatment of the group. These meetings were also used as a forum to discuss our own political views, including our attitudes to violence.

The house-mother and field-workers were also interviewed. The latter had worked not only with the Leandra group but with large numbers of displaced youth from different areas in the country.

Their perceptions of the youth, the reasons for their involvement in the struggle, the problems they felt the youth experienced, as well as their views on the future of the youth, were probed.

At the three year follow-up, approximately 40 per cent of the group, or 25 individuals (8 girls and 17 boys), were interviewed, either by the author assisted by a translator, or by a trained co-researcher who knew the format of the interview. These semi-structured interviews aimed at assessing the subjective and objective processes whereby individuals were inducted into the struggle, their key experiences, and the factors that sustained them in it. The interview also aimed at assessing individuals' reflections upon the 1984–86 period, their current political involvement, as well as their attitudes toward the role of violence. Their own exposure to violence was assessed, and some attempt was made to evaluate the consequences of this.

All interviews were recorded. In the end there were approximately 300 hours of interviews which were analysed. In addition, information was gleaned from key informants who knew the Leandra group very well. This information served as collateral information on the group members who were interviewed; data was also collected on the 35 individuals who were not interviewed at the time of follow-up. Basic demographic data was ascertained concerning factors such as employment, schooling, and current levels of political involvement.

The distillation which is given in my book is essentially my own, although it has been read and edited by a number of the counsellors and others who have had contact with either the Leandra group or other groups of displaced activists. In presenting what is essentially a personal distillation of material in a qualitative, descriptive fashion, the methodology of Jay Lifton in his work on Vietnam War veterans, Hiroshima victims and Nazi doctors is followed. In this work Lifton underlines the validity of 'articulated subjectivity or the use of the self as an investigative instrument' in the psychological enterprise (Lifton, 1973, p. 21).

In presenting his work, Lifton is clear that he is not acting as a neutral screen. He is engaged with his subjects with the totality of his being. That this does not detract from the value of his work which attempts to 'bring passion to investigation and scholarship to political and ethical stands' (Lifton, 1973, p. 16) is clear from the clarity and originality of the insights he generates. His works are undoubtedly classics in the field.

Similarly, in writing this book, I cannot claim to be neutral. My sympathies clearly lie with the youth, although I have not shared their lives, other than as a clinician or researcher. In this sense the observations presented are necessarily those made from the position of an outsider, filtered through lenses informed by my own background in general and my training in psychology in particular.

In presenting the data, the case-study format was used for a number of reasons. Firstly, it is in the nature of psychology that some appreciation of the general is obtained through an understanding of the particular. Secondly, in a time such as the present, when death, injury, pain and distress are being generated on an unprecedented scale, it seems important to individualise this and to stress that each statistic has a name, a face and a family. The case-study method emphasises this.

The case vignettes presented, however, do not depict individuals. They represent classic examples of the kinds of people who were activists in Leandra in 1984–86. The vignettes were informed by all the data, including that collected at the time of Wilgespruit, but they relied most heavily on the follow-up interviews which were more systematic and thorough. Each individual case-study was constructed from case material drawn from a number of persons who fitted the particular class of individual to be described, namely leader, follower, casualty or anti-social person. This style of presentation was necessary in order to protect confidentiality and to ensure each subject's security – crucial considerations in this study. Multiple precautions were therefore taken to protect the true identity of the subjects. When the original case material was processed, the real names of the subjects were deleted and they were given code names by key informants. When subjects were followed up, they were introduced by the key informants by their code names. Key informants whose real names were known were not interviewed themselves. Furthermore, they were not permitted to sit in on any of the interviews and thus were not aware of any disclosures whatsoever by other subjects.

The protection of the confidentiality of subjects is always of primary concern to researchers, but in these particular circumstances it was vitally important, hence the construction of composite vignettes rather than the presentation of actual case studies.

In this study it was clear that individual levels of functioning fluctuated over time. Members who had been in leadership positions dropped out, others who had been followers took their places.

Some consolidated their positions, some broke down. Despite these fluctuations and despite the diversity in the group, it seemed useful in presenting the data to do so with reference to four sub-groups which could be identified, bearing in mind that individuals might in the span of the research change category several times and that the categories themselves were fluid. The sub-groups identified were the leaders, the followers, the anti-social group and the psychological casualties. The following criteria were used at the time of follow-up to place individuals within these sub-groups.

Individuals were considered to be leaders if they occupied leadership positions both at the time of Wilgespruit and at the time of follow-up. Approximately 10 per cent of the group met these criteria.

Individuals who fell into the anti-social group or the tsotsi–comtsotsi group were placed in this group at the time of follow-up. They could be differentiated from the leaders along a number of dimensions, both personal and familial. Individuals were considered to be anti-social if they were identified as such by two key informants. The criteria agreed upon by the key informants in placing individuals in the anti-social category were participation in petty crime, gangsterism, harassment or intimidation of the community for personal gain. Members of the anti-social group who indulged in crime, harassment or intimidation under the guise of political intervention were termed 'comtsotsis'. Individuals who did not invoke such justifications were simply termed 'tsotsis'. These terms are commonly used in the townships, so they seemed to be most appropriate to use in this study.

Approximately ten per cent of the group were identified by the key informants to be tsotsis or comtsotsis, using these criteria. A further twenty per cent of the sample were identified as substance abusers in that their substance-abuse occurred at least twice a week on a regular basis to the extent that it interfered with their functioning. This criterion was suggested by the key informants themselves. The substance abusers and the tsotsi–comtsotsi group showed great overlap. Many tsotsis–comtsotsis were substance abusers although not all substance abusers were tsotsis or comtsotsis. In classifying individuals, the category of comtsotsi was given precedence over that of substance abuser. Individuals who indulged in anti-social behaviour as well as substance-abuse were classified in the tsotsi–comtsotsi group. Individuals who were substance abusers but who also showed signs of clinical symptomatology were placed in the substance-abuse group.

Individuals who in the follow-up interview showed clinical symptoms sufficient to disrupt their everyday life at the time of follow-up were termed clinical casualties. These individuals showed signs on interview of depression, anxiety, post-traumatic stress disorder or psychosomatic symptomatology at a level at which it was impairing functioning in everyday life. Of the 25 individuals interviewed at follow-up, 5 were placed in this category.

The 'follower' category was formed by default. Individuals who did not qualify for any of the other categories were classed as followers. Altogether 40 per cent of the group fell into this category. Within this category, however, there were several sub-divisions which were elaborated upon in the text.

Bibliography

Allen, V. 1970. Toward understanding riots: Some perspectives. *Journal of Social Issues*. 26. 1-18.

American Psychiatric Association. 1987. *Diagnostic and Statistical Manual (DSM III-R)*. Washington: American Psychiatric Association.

Anthony, E. & Cohler, B. 1987. *The invulnerable child*. New York: Guildford.

Anthony, E. 1987. Risk, vulnerability and resilience: An overview. In E. Anthony & B. Cohler (eds). *The invulnerable child*. New York: Guildford. 3-49.

Antonovsky, A. 1987. *Unraveling the mystery of health: How people manage stress and stay well*. San Francisco: Jassuy Bass Publishers.

Aries, P. 1962. *Centuries of childhood*. Middlesex: Penguin.

Bettelheim, B. 1979. *Surviving and other essays*. New York: A. Knopf.

Bion, W. 1961. *Experiences in groups and other papers*. London: Tavistock.

Bulhan, H. 1980. Frantz Fanon: The revolutionary psychiatrist. *Race and Class*. XXI. 3. 251-271.

Bulhan, H. 1985. *Frantz Fanon and the psychology of oppression*. New York: Plenum Press.

Campbell, J. 1956. *The hero with a thousand faces*. New York: Meridian.

Caplan, N. & Paige, J. 1968. A study of ghetto rioters. *Scientific American*. August. 15-21.

Charney, I. 1986. Genocide and mass destruction: Doing harm to others as a missing dimension in psychopathology. *Psychiatry*. 49. 144-157.

Cobbett, W. & Cohen, R. (eds.). 1988. *Popular struggles in South Africa*. London: J. Currey.

Cohler, B. 1987. Adversity, resilience and the study of lives. In E. Anthony & B. Cohler (eds). *The invulnerable child*. New York: Guildford. 363-424.

Collins, R. 1974. *Three faces of cruelty: Towards a comparative sociology of violence*. San Diego: University of California.

Davis, G. 1991. Gangs thrive in miasma of mistrust. *Weekly Mail*. 11-17 January.

Dawes, A. 1986. Politics and mental health: The position of clinical psychology in South Africa. *South African Journal of Psychology*. 10. 55-61.

Detainees' Parents Support Committee. 1986. *A memorandum on children under repression*. Johannesburg: DPSC.

Earls, F., Beardslee, W. & Garrison, W. 1987. Correlates and indicators of competence in young children. In E. Anthony & B. Cohler (eds). *The invulnerable child*. New York: Guildford. 70-83.

Fanon, F. 1963. *The wretched of the earth*. Middlesex: Penguin.

Festinger, L., Pepitane, A. & Newcomb, T. 1952. Some consequences of deindividuation in a group. *Journal of Abnormal and Social Psychology*. 47. 382-389.

Foster, D. 1991. Social influence III: Crowds and collective violence. In D. Foster & J. Louw-Potgieter (eds). *Social psychology in South Africa*. Johannesburg: Lexicon Publishers. 441-483.

Fraiberg, S. 1984. *Magic years: Understanding and handling the problems of early childhood*. New York: Scribner.

Freud, A. 1958. Adolescence. *The Psychoanalytic Study of the Child*. 13. 255-278.

Freud, S. 1913. *Totem and Taboo*. London: Hogarth Press.

Freud, S. 1919. *Introduction to Psycho-analysis and the war neuroses*. London: Hogarth Press.

Freud, S. 1925. *General works*. London: Imago Publishing.

Freud, S. 1921. Group therapy and the analysis of the ego. In S. Freud. 1985. *Civilisation, society and religion*. Middlesex: Pelican Books.

Freud, S. 1985. Why war. In *Civilisation, society and religion*. Middlesex: Pelican Books.

Freud, A. & Burlingham, D. 1943. *War and children*. London: Medical War Books.

Garmezy, N. 1983. Stressors of childhood. In N. Garmezy & M. Rutter (eds). *Stress, coping and development in children*. New York: McGraw Hill. 43-85.

Garmezy, N. 1990. The adaptation of children to a world at war. Paper presented at the conference on Children-in-War. Jerusalem. June 1990.

Garmezy, N. & Rutter, M (eds). 1983. *Stress, coping and development in children*. New York: McGraw Hill.

Gibson, K. 1987. Children in political violence. *Social Science and Medicine*. 28, 7. 659-667.

Gqubule, T. 1989. I go back to school. *Weekly Mail*. 2-9 June.

Gumede, M. 1990. *Traditional healers*. Johannesburg: Skotaville.

Gurr, T. 1970. *Why men rebel*. New Jersey: Princeton University Press.

Hammond-Tooke, D. 1990. *Rituals and medicine*. Johannesburg: Donker.

Haysom, N. 1983. *Mabangalala: The rise of right-wing vigilantes in South Africa*. Johannesburg.

Hietanen, A. 1983. The militarisation of children: Some trends. In M. Kahnert, D. Pitt & I. Taipale (eds). *Children and war*. Proceedings of symposium in Finland. March 1983. 188-198.

James, W. 1910. The moral equivalent of war. In P. Mayer (ed.). 1966. *The pacifist conscience*. Middlesex: Penguin.

Kagan, J. 1983. Stress and coping in early development. In N. Garmezy & M. Rutter (eds). *Stress, coping and development in children*. New York: McGraw Hill. 191-216.

Kahnert, M., Pitt D. & Taipale, I. 1983. *Children in war*. Proceedings of symposium at Siuntio Baths, Finland. March 1983.

Kelman, H. 1973. Violence without moral restraint: Reflections on the dehumanisation of victims and victimisers. *Journal of Social Issues*. 29. 25-61.

Kerner, O. 1968. *Report of the Advisory Committee on Civil Disorders*. New York: Bantam.

La Hausse, 1990. The cows and Nongoloza: Youth, crime and amalaita gangs in Durban, 1900-1936. *Journal of Southern African Studies*. 16, 1. 79-111.

Lambert, T. & Webster, E. 1988. The re-emergence of political unionism in contemporary South Africa. In W. Cobbett & R. Cohen (eds). *Popular struggles in South Africa*. London: J. Currey.

Laufer, R. 1988. The serial self. In J. Wilson, J. Harel & B. Kahana (eds). *Human adaptation to extreme stress*. New York: Plenum Press.

The Lawyers Committee for Human Rights. 1986. *The war against children: South Africa's youngest victims*. New York.

Levi, P. 1988. *If this is a man*. London: Abacus, 1988.

Lifton, J. 1973. *Home from the war: Vietnam veterans neither victims nor executioners*. New York: Touchstone, Simon and Schuster.

Maluleke, D.G. 1989. A study of the motives of black adolescent participants in the school boycotts in a black urban area: A humanistic perspective. Unpublished M.A. dissertation. University of the Witwatersrand, Johannesburg.

Manganyi, N. C. 1990. Crowds and their vicissitudes: Psychology and law in the South African court-room. In N. C. Manganyi & A. du Toit (eds). *Political violence and the struggle in South Africa*. Johannesburg: Southern Publishers.

Mansfield, 1982. *The gestalts of war*. New York: Dial Press.

Miller, A. 1988. *For your own good*. New York: Farrar Straus and Giroux.

Moss, G. 1987. Court briefings. *Work in Progress*. 48. 36-37.

Mtshali, M. 1982. *Give us a break: Diaries of a group of Soweto children*. Braamfontein: Skotaville Publishers.

Munich, R. & Astrachan, B. 1983. Group dynamics. In H. Kaplan & B. Sadock (eds). *Comprehensive group psychotherapy*. London: Williams & Wilkins. 15-23.

Murphy, L. 1987. Further reflections on resilience. In E. Anthony & B. Cohler (eds). *The invulnerable child*. New York: Guildford. 84-105.

Myers, D. 1988. *Social Psychology*. 2nd ed. New York: McGraw Hill.

Noyes, R. & Kletti, R. 1976. Depersonalisation in the face of life threatening danger: An interpretation. *Omega*. 7. 103-113.

Platter, D. 1983. Protection of children in international humanitarian law. In M. Kahnert, D. Pitt & I. Taipale (eds). *Children and war*. Proceedings of symposium in Finland. March 1983. 198-214.

Peck, E. 1987. The traits of true invulnerability and post-traumatic stress in psychoanalysed men of action. In E. Anthony & B. Cohler (eds). *The invulnerable child*. 315-360.

Punamaki, R. 1983. Psychological reactions of Palestinian and Israeli children to war and violence. In M. Kahnert, D. Pitt & I Taipale, *Children and war*. Proceedings of symposium at Siuntio Baths, Finland.

Raphael, B. 1986. *When disaster strikes*. London: Hutchinson.

Reicher, S. 1987. Crowd behaviour as social action. In J. C. Turner (ed). *Rediscovering the social group: A self categorisation theory.* Oxford: Blackwell. 171-202.

Reynolds, P. 1989. Children of tribulation: The need to heal and the means to heal war trauma. Paper presented at the Fourth International Workshop – Ethnography of Childhood. 23-26 July 1989. Victoria Falls.

Richter, L. 1990. Wretched childhoods: The challenge to psychological theory and practice. Inaugural lecture, University of South Africa, Pretoria. 15 March 1990.

Rosenhan, H. 1972. Pro-social behaviour of children. In W. Hartup (ed). *The young child* (Vol. 2). Washington D.C.: National Association for the Education of Young Children. 340-359.

Rutter, M. 1981. *Maternal deprivation reassessed.* Middlesex: Penguin Books.

Sartre, J. 1963. Introduction. In F. Fanon. 1963. *Wretched of the earth.* Middlesex: Penguin.

Schilder, P. 1953. *Medical psychology.* New York: International Universities Press.

Setiloane, C. W. M. 1990. *A study of attitudes towards, and tolerance of, violence by a group of schoolchildren.* Unisa: Institute for Behavioural Sciences. Internal Report. IBS 90/14.

Shatan, C. 1977. Bogus manhood, bogus honour: Surrender and transfiguration in the U.S. marine corp. *Psychological Review.* 64. 585-610.

Shorter, A. 1985. *Jesus and the witchdoctor: An approach to healing and wholeness.* New York: Orbis Books.

Silver, S. & Wilson, J. 1988. Native American healing and purification rituals of war stress. In J. Wilson, J. Harel & B. Kahana (eds). *Human adaptation to extreme stress.* New York: Plenum Press.

Slater, P. 1966. *Microcosm: Structural, psychological and religious evolution in groups.* New York: John Wiley and Sons.

South African Institute of Race Relations. 1977. *A survey of race relations in South Africa: 1976.* SAIRR: Johannesburg.

Straker, G. & Sanctuaries Counselling Team. 1987a. The continuous traumatic stress syndrome – the single therapeutic interview. *Psychology in Society.* 8. 48-79.

Straker, G. & Sanctuaries Counselling Team. 1988. Apartheid and child abuse. *Psychology in Society.* 9. 3-13.

Straker, G. 1988. Child abuse, counselling and apartheid: The work of the Sanctuary Counselling Team. *Free Associations.* 14. 7-39.

Straker, G., Moosa, F. and Sanctuaries Counselling Team. 1988. Post-traumatic stress disorder: A reaction to state-supported child abuse and neglect. *Child Abuse and Neglect.* 12. 383-395.

Straker, G. 1989. From victim to villain: A 'slight' of speech? Media representations of township youth. *South African Journal of Psychology.* 19, 1. 20-27.

Swartz, L. & Levett, A. 1989. Political repression and children in South Africa: The social construction of damaging effects. *Social Science and Medicine.* 28. 741-750.

Swilling, M. 1988. The United Democratic Front and township revolt. In W. Cobbett & R. Cohen (eds). *Popular struggles in South Africa.* London:

J. Currey. 90-113.

Tomlinson, T. 1968. The development of a riot ideology among urban Negroes. *The American Behavioral Scientist*. March–April. 28-31.

Turton, R., Straker, G. & Moosa, F. 1991. Experiences of violence in the lives of township youths in 'unrest' and 'normal' conditions. *South African Journal of Psychology*. In press.

Ulman, R. & Brothers, D. 1988. *The shattered self: A psychoanalytic study of trauma*. London: The Analytic Press.

Index

Index of names cited